How to Fall Out of Love

Dr. Debora Phillips
with Robert Judd

How to Fall
Out of Love

Introduction by Joseph Wolpe, M.D.

Houghton Mifflin Company
Boston 1978

Library of Congress Cataloging in Publication Data

Phillips, Debora.
　How to fall out of love.

　Includes index.
　1. Love.　2.　Behavior therapy.　I.　Judd, Robert, joint author.　II.　Title.
BF575.L8P47　　158'.2　　78-16908
ISBN 0-395-27116-9

Printed in the United States of America

W 10 9 8 7 6 5 4 3 2 1

To my patients and friends, whose problems in being human have led me to seek solutions.

"I trust all joy"
— *Theodore Roethke*

Foreword and Acknowledgments

It's ironic that our great source of joy, love, could cause such pain. Now that half the marriages in the United States will end in divorce and now that casual affairs are common, there seems to be an almost parallel rise in suffering. Perhaps as choices increase and rigid behavior codes decline, anxiety rises. Perhaps people are simply more open about their pain. But whatever the reason, every time I mention that I have a program called "Falling Out of Love," I am swamped with letters and phone calls and personal visits from people who have seen the order of their lives made chaotic, who experience emotional devastation and trauma, and who desperately need help.

Hence this book. It is a painstaking reproduction of an extraordinarily successful behavior therapy program. And it is for the millions of people who are suffering and have no idea how to deal with that suffering other than vaguely trying to suppress what they feel: love for someone who does not love them, or love for someone in a relationship that gives them only pain.

How to Fall Out of Love is a sincere effort to make therapy practical, concrete, accessible, brief and durable. The point is to stop the pain caused by obsessive thinking about someone who does not or cannot love you. And to give you the skills to build a new relationship.

In many important ways, *How to Fall Out of Love* is the result of some fifty years of countless scientific observations on the learning process by scientists from Pavlov to Wolpe. So I want first to acknowledge my debt to a very substantial body of knowledge, called behavior therapy, which has been gained through an extraordinary expenditure of time and effort in the laboratory and in clinical therapeutic practice.

Moreover, and more important, this is in many ways Joseph Wolpe's book. (At least the best of it is. Its shortcomings and inaccuracies are my own.) As the father and founder of behavior therapy, he has made a substantial contribution to healing the pain of human suffering. As my teacher, he has led me to enormous possibilities. And I want to thank both Joe and Stella Wolpe for their constant personal support and for many specific contributions to the manuscript. And I'd like to thank David Wolpe for suggesting the terms "graduated calming" and "silent ridicule."

Those who know the Reverend Doctor William Kirby as Bill will recognize many of his ideas and concepts throughout the book. And I want to add my recognition, gratitude and appreciation for his personal support and guidance, and for teaching me so much.

I want to thank Jean Firstenberg and Paul Firstenberg for their love and support and treasured advice, and for helping me realize the potential in my work.

And thank you also to:

Professor Nancy Weiss, whose excellent suggestions and sensitivity at many stages of the manuscript had a profound influence on the finished book.

Dr. Michael Ascher, who helped me develop silent ridicule.

Carol Thompson, for her wisdom, sanity, judgment, humor and a prodigious amount of hard work and sound advice.

Marie Luisi, for backstage wisdom and up-front kindness, and for introducing me to Bob Judd.

William Phillips, for support and for patience and help with the manuscript. Maxwell Anderson said Bill could be a writer instead of a scientist. He is a wise and loving man in either case.

Bob Judd, for making this book possible; for his enthusiastic understanding of behavior therapy; for his tireless patience; for translating awkward clinical language into eloquent and accessible prose. And for never asking me to compromise in order to popularize.

David Harris, a gentle editor with a razor mind, who pruned the awkward constructions, gave the book shape and form and freely gave us help from the start.

Special acknowledgment goes to Teresa Holeman and Aurelia Bolling, who make my work possible.

DEBORA PHILLIPS

Contents

CONTENTS

Introduction

How to Fall Out of Love is based on behavior therapy. Behavior therapy, a modern psychotherapy grounded in scientific knowledge about learning, proceeds from the basic assumption that nearly all human behavior is learned. Relearning through methods developed by behavior therapists can enable people to change behavior that causes them pain.

Behavior therapy applies experimentally established principles of learning to change unadaptive behavior. Unadaptive behavior includes unadaptive feelings like jealousy, fear of rejection, fear of intimacy, fear of authority figures; as well as functional problems like overeating or sexual problems. Behavior therapy weakens behavior that causes you anxiety or hinders your ability to function comfortably in your own environment; it strengthens behavior that helps you pursue the life you want to live. Emotional problems can be cured — not merely controlled, or coped with, or understood, but fundamentally removed.

Because emotional behavior is learned at a primitive (subcortical) level of neural organization, changing it must involve the same primitive level. No matter how clearly you may see that a particular emotional behavior is unhelpful to you, rational insight alone will not equip you to behave in a different fashion. Emotional habits are resistant to logical argument or good advice, because something that is learned emotionally cannot be dealt with purely at an intellectual level.

Anxiety is the central component of much unadaptive behavior. Anxiety itself is learned behavior. As a result of certain past experiences, an individual forms the habit of reacting automatically with anxiety or fear to certain situations. In some circumstances the fear is appropriate because real danger is involved. In cases where no real danger exists, the fear or anxiety is inappropriate (a fear of heights while looking out of a window would be an inappropriate fear). For some people such anxiety — whether fear of flying, fear of heights, fear of rejection, fear of what others think, fear of taking risks, fear of criticism, fear of intimacy, or a whole range of sexual fears — can become so debilitating that it seriously interferes with daily life.

Anxiety reduction is central to behavior therapy. The elimination of anxiety is most easily accomplished by inhibiting the anxiety with a competing response. If a therapist can evoke a response (for example, deep relaxation) in the presence of a stimulus that provokes anxiety (for example, criticism from your father), the bond between the old stimulus and the anxiety it caused (for example, fear of criticism) will be weakened. Eliminating or significantly reducing the anxiety removes the impediments to creative and comfortable functioning in daily living.

This book illustrates the way behavior therapy deals with certain complex spectra of human responses — emotional involvements that have outlived their appropriateness. People who are depressed or oppressed by obsessive thinking about another person will learn how to use competing thoughts to break their repetitive chains of thought. People who are habitually dominated by others will learn how to overcome feelings of helplessness by learning to be assertive. People who are consumed with jealousy will learn how to vanquish the green-eyed monster. Those who have difficulty socially, or need to develop skills of intimacy, will find help and guidance. However, the primary function of this book is to stop the pain of not being loved, and to help people build new relationships when old ones have broken down. It has all the virtues of behavior therapy: brevity, action, a systematic, step-by-step program to reach specific goals. It demonstrates one of the great strengths of behavior therapy — dealing with large, complex emotional difficulties in manageable component parts. Moreover, its clarity, warmth, and understanding make the techniques of behavior therapy both accessible and useful to the general reader.

JOSEPH WOLPE, M.D.
Professor of Psychiatry, Temple University
School of Medicine, Philadelphia, Pennsylvania

PART ONE

How to Fall
Out of Love...

1

The First Step

There are millions of people who are in love and in pain because their love is not returned. Chances are, several people you know are going through the painful process of falling out of love.

Suddenly, without warning, a young husband leaves his wife to live with another woman. A graduate student is deserted by his fiancée just before their wedding. An elderly woman's husband dies. A secretary is in love with her boss who strings her along. A waitress is having an affair with a teacher but doesn't want to damage her marriage. A schoolboy has an obsessive longing for his dead father. A young woman banker falls in love with a client who cannot return her love. A nurse is in love with an alcoholic. A businessman's fiancée is a chronic liar. A love affair ends for the photographer but not for the model.

Our whole culture is geared and meshed to help us fall in love, but nowhere are there signs to point the way out.

Falling out of love is usually a natural, although painful, process. Most people can and do fall out of love without help. Time heals, they meet other people and their lives go on. On the other hand, for some of us the loss of a love can be almost overwhelming — an obsession, an intense, enduring, immobilizing pain. Being in love when it's not returned can lead to depression, obsessive thoughts, sexual   3 dysfunction, inability to work, difficulty in making friends, and self-destructiveness. For all sorts of reasons, some of us hold fast to the memory of love as if it were the real thing. Love's so precious (real love, false love or any kind of love) that we fear to let go, afraid of the great void that comes in the aftermath, the loneliness, the feelings of rejection and the anguish.

People who come to my office for help are in love and in pain. I'm a behavior therapist and what I do is help stop the pain so you can escape from a nonproductive dreamworld of unreturned love. So you can love again, and be loved.

I first began developing this particular program three years ago in response to a young woman whose partner had suddenly left without warning or explanation.

•

Marjorie, twenty-four-year-old graduate student. She had been living for two years with a male graduate student. Both planned to be field anthropologists after graduation. They shared courses, friends and vacations and they planned to be married shortly after graduation. The day of graduation, Marjorie's fiancé left (for his parents' home in Nebraska, it was later learned) without a word of explanation. The more she thought about what had happened and why, the more she became obsessed and depressed. After two weeks she couldn't bring herself to apply for grants or for a university job. She felt isolated, she felt she was to blame, and she felt so depressed she seldom left her room. Marjorie was highly skeptical of therapy, but she was also becoming increasingly anxious about what was happening to her life, so, at the urging of a friend, she agreed to see me. I designed a plan of action for her. The first step was thought-stopping to reduce the excessive amount of time she spent thinking about him. Next she practiced silent ridicule to put him in a more realistic and less perfect light. And finally she embarked on a program of positive image building to repair the damage that had been done to her own self-image and to realize her own importance and value.

Marjorie's thoughts of her former lover dropped from approximately sixty-five per day in the first week to two to four per day at the end of the second week. In the third week she began applying for grants for field work at an anthropological site in Mexico. She stopped therapy at the end of the third week.

Follow-up: Marjorie accepted a grant for field work in Iran, is not married (does not want to be, she says), and describes herself as being in "great shape."

•

Marjorie's rapid response was by no means unusual, as numbers of other people who successfully went through the program were later to prove. Young, old, men, women, gay, straight . . . they were all, in some ways, immobilized by the pain. Many of them had a healthy skepticism in regard to therapy in general and to a systematic program in particular. I say healthy skepticism because some therapy can take years and still produce little in the way of results. And any preset program might seem too rigid, generalized, cold and mechanical to deal with your own complex, unique and private feelings of love.

And yet, there are advantages to a systematic program, important advantages. It really does help to observe and organize your feelings. It helps because once you observe your feelings, you objectify them, gain perspective and therefore begin to change them. It also helps to have a step-by-step program of positive things to do rather than struggle with a tide of amorphous, overwhelming feelings. And it helps to have specific goals so you can measure your progress.

The program in this book is behavior therapy. That is, it is based on what neurologists, behaviorists and other scientists have found out in the laboratory about the way we 5 learn. So it's not a pep talk for following moral guidelines or achieving more insights; it is a straightforward positive program based on observed facts. I developed the program at Temple University Medical School (where I am on the faculty) and at Princeton University. Thus far, it has been enormously successful. By that I mean that those who have gone through the program to date have fallen out of love in the sense that they no longer constantly think about the person they formerly loved, no longer feel great pain and longing when they do think of that person, and are able to build new relationships with new people. Some of the techniques and exercises may seem drastic to you at first glance. So I should emphasize that no matter how strong the technique may seem, you won't end up feeling anger or hostility or hatred toward the person you want to fall out of love with. I am not attempting to shift your feelings to the opposite of love. I am aiming at the great middle ground of indifference.

What I would like to do first is give you an overview of the program and explain a little about how it works.

First and foremost, falling in love is not a rational process. It's not planned or reasoned. There are countless definitions of what love is. And certainly the experience of a teen-ager whose sweetheart has moved away is different in many ways from the widower whose wife of forty years has just died. But however you define love, I believe that if you feel you are in love, you are. Love is simply too individual and subjective to fit into any simple or objective definition.

Falling in love is an intense emotional and intuitive experience. A lot of it is magic and chemistry. Because falling in love is emotionally learned, it has to be emotionally unlearned if you are going to fall out of love. That is why insights, rational thinking and exploring the reasons you fell in love are all inefficient and ineffective. The whys of your love can be intriguing. But it is unlikely that knowing them will help you stop the pain of being in love with someone

6

who does not love you. The first, most important thing that you should do is ask yourself if you want to stop the pain. And the way you stop that pain is not by talking about it or by looking for insights or finding insights. It is by dealing with that pain in a direct, systematic way.

What you feel about someone is largely in response to that person — complex responses to the things they've done and said, to the way they look and feel, to the things you have done and said. These are learned responses. You didn't feel them about that person before you knew what that person looked and felt like, before you'd talked and done things together. Over a period of time those responses become deeply ingrained among the patterns of your mind. Constantly thinking about that person, constantly repeating fixed images of him or her can reinforce those images and make them stronger and more persistent.

The love you feel for that person is learned on many levels. That fact — that the love you feel for that person is something you have *learned* to feel for that person — is tremendously important. Because if you learned to love, you can unlearn that love.

If you can learn to unlearn, what freedom! You won't have to spend years struggling in the backwash of an old love affair or, for example, the death of a wife. You won't have to rely on illuminating the whys and wherefores of your life with insight. If love is learned and if you can unlearn to love someone because you want to stop the pain, you won't have to rely on wishful thinking ("if only, if only, if only"), the advice of friends or outsiders, or the random chance of inspiration or insight, or the slow passage of time. You can do it yourself — now.

Let's start with a survey of the contents of *How to Fall Out of Love*. It begins with thought-stopping, a technique developed by the father of behavior therapy, Dr. Joseph Wolpe, a professor of psychiatry at Temple University School of Medicine.

Thought-stopping was one of the early innovations of behavior therapy and it remains one of the most powerful. In many ways it is the foundation for the chapters that follow. Thought-stopping takes you that first essential step away from being in love; that is, it reduces the time you spend thinking about that person, and leaves you more time for yourself and other people. Thought-stopping itself is a reasonably simple exercise, but it has all the hallmarks of behavior therapy: a specific goal, the suppression of one response by a competing response, action, brevity, a means for measuring progress, simplicity and a functional practicality. Which is to say, it works.

The second step, silent ridicule, is designed to make falling out of love easier. Thought-stopping reduces the frequency of your thoughts of the person you love; next, silent ridicule, a new technique that was developed by Dr. Michael Ascher (Associate Professor of Psychiatry at Temple University Medical School) and me, reduces the intensity of those thoughts. It seems that one of our most human traits is to idealize someone who can't or won't return our love. Silent ridicule uses humor to erode that pedestal you've so kindly built for the person you love. It is also an especially useful technique if you find you have to see that person from time to time.

After you've reduced the frequency and intensity of thoughts of that person, you can turn your attention to yourself. You are especially vulnerable now, and depression and doubt make poor companions. Your own self-view can realistically improve with a little perspective, so another chapter presents a series of positive exercises (more unlearning) to help develop your strength to stand alone if you need to, along with the courage to meet other people and build bridges to new relationships.

The point is that each chapter takes you further from your former love. And it also takes you closer to more meaningful, rewarding relationships with others. So you can go as far or as short a distance as you like. The program continues through desensitization (as created by Dr. Wolpe) for dealing with jealousy and rejection; covert sensitization, which I call repulsion, developed by Dr. Joseph Cautela (behavior therapist, Boston College); orgasmic reconditioning, developed by Dr. John Marquis (psychologist in Palo Alto, California); positive reinforcement as developed by Dr. B. F. Skinner (psychologist, Harvard University); and many useful skills for developing warmth and intimacy with a new person.

So instead of struggling with the shadows of your past or trying to decide who's to blame or why this or that happened, or even why you feel the way you do, each chapter is a step away from an old relationship as well as a positive step toward developing new ones.

2

Thought-Stopping

Most people who are in love with someone but are not loved in return find it difficult to stop loving that person. But chances are they, or you, would like to think about that person less. What you have to do is unlearn some of those things you've learned to think and feel about that person.

All your life you have been learning. From the time you were born until now, you have been learning emotionally, intellectually and physically. It would take months or years to remember and evaluate all the things you've learned to feel about, say, your mother and your father, not to mention your teachers and friends and all the other important people in your life. So let's ignore everyone else for now and concentrate on just one person — the person you love.

Stop.

Stop thinking about that person.

Chances are you've already said to yourself that you have to stop thinking about the person you love. You may even have told yourself that hundreds of times. It doesn't work, does it?

It's also irritating to have friends tell you to stop thinking about that person. ("She's not worth it." "You should know better." "Cheer up," and so on.) The mind seems almost too contrary to do what it's told, as if it had a mind of its own. For example, if I told you not to think of Attila the

Hun for the next sixty seconds . . . in the next sixty seconds you're probably going to find at least one Hun on horseback riding through your thoughts.

Chasing Attila the Hun out of your thoughts is easy compared to getting the person you love out of the kingdom of your mind. Because there are so many sweet, delicious things to think about. So many conversations left unfinished. So many private, tender things. It's hard to stop thinking those thoughts. They are specific, repetitive and often very, very forceful. But they can be stopped through a systematic behavioral program.

You can train a thought to stay away. You can starve a thought. Allowing a thought to come back time and again is to feed it, reinforce it, make it grow stronger, and, in some cases, more painful. Thought patterns about someone you love can become so strong that making up your mind to stop thinking about them often isn't enough. You need to actively, systematically inhibit those thoughts. And you need new thoughts to put in place of them.

Make a list.

Make a list of the best, most positive scenes and pleasures you can think of that do not involve that person.

The point is that everything you have learned, including your emotional responses to that person, has a neurological center. On a very basic level, many neurons in your nervous system have a double link. One link excites an action or emotion. Another link inhibits other actions or emotions. In physical terms, for example, the neurons that order your thigh to tighten also, at the same time, inhibit the muscles at the back of your leg from tightening. It has been hypothesized and proven that this double link of action/inhibition also exists emotionally. Love inhibits hate. Laughter is inhibited by sadness, anger or anxiety. And laughter, in turn, can inhibit sadness, anger and anxiety. (While the neurological mechanics of our emotions are just now revealing themselves to neurologists, the phenomenon was 11 noted as far back as 1673 by the philosopher Spinoza, who said in *Ethics*, "An emotion can only be controlled or destroyed by another emotion contrary thereto, and with more power for controlling emotion.")

Therefore, make a list of scenes, places, events and/or feelings that are wholly pleasurable to you, but do not involve the person you need to stop thinking about. Your list is entirely your own. No one else need ever see it. And the act of writing down the list helps you to become involved with pleasure without being involved with your former love.

It may be helpful to you to see some other lists, even though they may not be anything like your own. First, the list of a nineteen-year-old college student in love with an older woman who did not love him.

•

Aaron, nineteen-year-old college student. Aaron said he was failing every subject, losing his friends and that he hated himself. He thought of Jane constantly, incessantly. They'd met because he was working for a contractor, building a garage behind her house. He saw her dressing one morning. And it became a movie in Aaron's mind that he could watch again and again: *He is on the rafters of the garage on an early summer morning. The sun is warm, the curtains flutter in an open window and Jane tosses in her bed. She wears a simple white nightgown. She's thrown the covers back. She sits up, raises the nightgown over her shoulders and drops it to the floor. She walks across the room. She looks out the window, nude, sleepy and pleased that the sky is blue. She sees Aaron looking at her. She smiles.* They met several times, had a few dates, made love a couple of times. But she wasn't really interested.

Aaron, of course, had several other specific Jane movies in his mind ready at all times for instant replay. While Aaron didn't want to argue about or be told about what was good for her, or him, he did see and feel that he was in real

12

pain. He could see that it was hurting his life. And he did agree to try to stop the pain by doing thought-stopping.

•

Aaron's List

1. The sweet, fat crack of the bat as you hit a home run in the World Series. Cheers, rounding the bases, TV contracts.
2. Finding a cool freshwater stream running into a beach in Mendocino, California.
3. Sitting at the kitchen table when you were six and watching your mother make supper.
4. Winning the Olympic marathon and going on, nonstop, to grab a pole, vault and set a new world record at twenty-one feet even. (When you go over the top you can feel the sun shine on the soles of your bare feet.)
5. Sliding your hand inside the bikini of the innocent MJ.
6. Liberating the stockade in Khartoum.
7. Your first screen test at MGM.
8. Rescuing Linda from a mugger. Graciously receiving her gratitude.
9. MJ's innocent hand sliding inside your pants.
10. Riding a moose into town.
11. Sailing out into the Pacific sunset on a three-masted, mahogany and teak schooner headed for Tahiti.

Here's another list from a thirty-one-year-old woman who had been living with a man for four years.

•

Laura, thirty-one-year-old writer. She had lived with a younger man for four years. While she worried about being over-weight, she was exceptionally bright, attractive, inventive and witty. He was unskilled, but she made enough money for both of them. She introduced him to her circle of   13 friends and gave him the money and encouragement to set up a men's clothing store. Just as he was beginning to be successful, he left her to live with a woman he met at a party. "I just fell in love with her," he said. Laura was in real torture. Just when he had become strong enough to stand on his own two feet, he'd left her. Why? Was she ugly? Unlovable? Had she given him too much? But most of all she profoundly missed him. All their friends knew them both. She felt cut in half. Kept reaching over to touch him in bed when he wasn't there. And she hated his new lover with fury and would not tolerate anyone who would not revile her new rival. We did thought-stopping (her writer's imagination made for a particularly rich, inventive list), silent ridicule (this was especially useful because she kept running into him at friends' houses or on the street or in restaurants), graduated calming (to deal with the jealousy she felt for the other woman), positive image building (so that she could know that she was an extraordinarily attractive woman), and finally, repulsion as a drastic but effective way of changing her view of him as the only possible man for her, ever.

Follow-up: Laura took much longer than most people. After four weeks she was still thinking of her former lover four to eight times a day. However, repulsion (which would not have worked earlier) finally put an end to her obsessive thinking about her former lover. And after six weeks she was able to see him and have dinner with him. And while "relaxed" would be an exaggeration, she was able to deal with the situation, and felt strong because of her self-control. One month later she formed another loving relationship.

•

Laura's List

1. A large silver platter of shaved ice. On the ice, blue point oysters, littleneck clams, and in the center, in a

large cut crystal bowl, fresh beluga caviar. There's more if you'd like. And cold Dom Perignon champagne to go with it.

2. As a young girl on a summer morning riding her bicycle down a steep straight dirt road. The dirt road has little ripples on the surface and pebbles. The bike is going at tremendous speed. She takes her hands off the handlebars and skitters downhill with the sun in her face.

3. Peter Ustinov is her masseur.

4. Robert Redford is his assistant.

5. Walking into an extravagant hotel, she is mistaken for a famous rock star. The drummer is insisting they sleep together now. Newspaper columnists want her advice.

6. Making love with a stranger on a hot afternoon in a farm field.

7. Riding on the back of a big motorcycle on a country road, with her arms around a man in a black leather jacket.

8. Holding hands with Peter Nelson in secret during the junior high school assembly when she was thirteen. Feeling his hand on her knee.

9. What to do with a year's free pass on Pan Am.

10. Inheriting a farm on a small island in Greece.

11. Walking in a deep pine forest and finding a deer that is tame.

Both Aaron and Laura's lists are unusually long. But they are useful here in showing you some of the variety of possibilities of pleasurable thoughts that do not involve your former love. The truth is, most people make a very short list, partly because they are depressed and thinking of pleasurable thoughts requires a lot of effort. And partly because they are so used to thinking about their lover that it's hard

15

to imagine a happy scene without that person in it. Here are a few lists of a more typical length:

•

Charles, thirty-four-year-old mechanic who was in love with a woman he'd met when she brought her car in for a tune-up. They were both married with children.

•

Charles's List

1. Country-fried chicken, yams, home fries, and a big slice of pecan pie.
2. Watching the lead skater in the ice show skate in the nude.

•

Tom, forty-eight-year-old science teacher whose wife had left him while they were on vacation in Yellowstone Park.

•

Tom's List

1. Catching a twelve-pound bass.
2. Finding a completely original, cobalt blue, tall Lincoln drape Aladdin kerosene lamp, still in its original box, for sale for five dollars in a junk store.
3. Swimming naked in the sea.

•

Melissa, a thirty-three-year-old librarian whose husband had died in a car crash.

•

Melissa's List

1. Watching the sun come up on a spring morning in the desert when the desert flowers are blooming.
16 2. Finishing a handmade mahogany chest she was making.

Seeing the deep red glow of the wood. The sharp, thin, new smell of the varnish.

•

Granger, a twenty-six-year-old market researcher who wanted to stop being in love with a married woman.

•

Granger's List

1. Telling his boss to shove it in great detail.

•

Another person liked to think of having lunch at a special Northern Italian restaurant. Another man liked to think of making love with different men under a waterfall in Yosemite National Park. Another man liked to think of vanilla ice cream.

•

The point is that your own list is your own. You may want to use a scene or two from the above lists, or you may well prefer scenes of your own. It doesn't have to be a funny list or a sexy one or a serious one, or even a long list. It doesn't have to be anything . . . only yours. You can be as outrageous or as plain as you like, nobody's watching.

It would be good if you'd write your list now . . .

Now that you have your list, purposely bring on a thought of the person you want to fall out of love with. The first microsecond that thought enters your mind, yell "STOP" as loudly as you can. (Don't allow the thought to develop. Don't allow the thought of that person to go on beyond the first glimmer of that thought.) And then, in the next instant bring on one of the best thoughts from your list. And whenever you happen spontaneously to think of that person, stop that thought by yelling "STOP" so that the thought cannot form in your mind. And then, instantly replace that thought with a thought from your list. 17

That, in a nutshell, is thought-stopping — actively inhibiting thoughts you want to go away. The goal is to reduce the time you spend thinking about that person. But thought-stopping is also an important exercise for another reason. It gives you more control so that you're not at the mercy of random thoughts and feelings.

•

Barbara, twenty-seven-year-old editor. She had been profoundly in love for five years with another editor at the same publishing house. He was married, but he said it was a loveless marriage. Barbara often thought of the quiet afternoons they spent working on a book together, making love in the sun on a blanket while on a picnic in the woods. She saw him every day at work. Each year he would tell her that their affair was making him feel too guilty and had to stop. He would not speak to her, except out of professional necessity. After a month he would come back saying he could not live without her. In the fifth year of their relationship, after he'd said they were, once again, "through," she'd had an abortion. The trauma of the experience made her realize that she was in a dead-end relationship. She decided that she did want a family and home of her own. However, she was deeply in love with him. She had come to hate going to work, found it difficult to leave her apartment on weekends, found she was moody, short-tempered with other people, and found that she was constantly thinking of the sensual afternoons they'd had together.

We began thought-stopping. She shut out thoughts of their lovemaking ("My hand prowling through the fur on his chest") and their intellectual discussions ("I wonder what he thinks of Randolph's new book?") with thoughts of the beautiful tropical fish in the Indian Ocean off the coast of Sri Lanka, making love with the UN ambassador, and of rich foods forbidden by her diet. In just two weeks of thought-stopping she found that she was thinking of him only two or three times a day on those days when she did not see him. She also did silent ridicule, positive image building, repulsion. After one month, she accepted his invitation to lunch. She felt some slight pangs of regret but also a very strong sense of strength and personal worth. She rejected his invitation to "begin all over again" and kept the conversation light and friendly. Shortly thereafter she stopped therapy.

Follow-up: She still works at the same publishing house. And is now married to another man.

•

Thought-stopping is a simple exercise, but it is all the more powerful for that. There's an old myth that anything worthwhile can only be achieved through sacrifice and pain. I think we know better now.

It does take time to do thought-stopping. But those thoughts of the person you love take your time too. They're worse than robbers; they're muggers who leave you bruised and hurt. And since you're so used to wallowing in them, it takes time and effort to weaken them.

And thought-stopping does take practice. Love is our most powerful positive emotion. For centuries theologians have said that God is love. And Tolstoy in *War and Peace* wrote: "Love is God and to die means that I, a particle of love, shall return to the general and eternal source." You can still hear the Beatles singing, "love, love, love, all you need is love," on the radio. And some 250 years ago, Isaac Watts wrote a fine hymn with the lines, "Love so amazing, so divine/Demands my soul, my life, my all." I'm mixing secular and holy love on purpose. There is so much love, so many kinds, so many qualities, that its beauty, force and power have dazzled writers and poets since the beginning of time. And no doubt as long as we have writers, poets or even two people left on earth, we shall hear more of love. Of course, you know all this. You know firsthand how powerful love is. Everyone this side of madness is "for" love. So unlearning the emotions and thoughts you have 19 learned as a response to your former love is hard. Those thoughts have built up tremendous momentum over time. And the thoughts from your list are probably new and not yet really as strong.

The difference in strength between thoughts of your former lover and thoughts from your list is a matter of conditioning, practice and time.

So it is hard at first. You may feel foolish, self-conscious, uncertain, hesitant, too tired, or any of the other dubious things that people feel when they first shout "STOP." It's entirely possible the thought won't go away the first time you try. You have to be persistent and try again.

One sixty-five-year-old woman in Ohio had to keep hammering at it, driving it out ten times before the thought of the man who had left her would go away the first day she tried thought-stopping. So don't expect it to be easy at first. It's simple, but not easy. However, as you practice it will become easier, and the thoughts of your former love will become weaker and less frequent until they stop coming in altogether. And the reason they will stop coming in altogether is threefold. First, when you keep a thought out you are unlearning — extinguishing that thought by refusing it the reinforcement of the repetition it needs for survival. Second, the pleasant replacement thought is a reward for stopping the thought. And thus, it reinforces the habit of *stopping* those negative thoughts. On a basic neurological level, you learn to stop thinking about that person. So the more you do it, the easier it gets and the better it works. Third, you are using competing thoughts to break repetition chains — replacing images of your old love with new competing images.

I strongly recommend that you keep a record of how many times a day you think of the person you love. Simply mark a card with the days of the week and place a tick beside the day each time you think of that person. It's an excellent way for you to measure your progress and to reinforce the thought-stopping process. Here, for example, is the card of a young man who was in love with another student who did not love him.

Wed. ///////////////////////////////////////
Thurs. ///////////////////////////////////////
Fri. ////////////////////////
Sat. //
Sun. ///
Mon. //////////////////////////////
Tues. //////////////////////
Wed. ////////////////
Thurs. //////////////////
Fri. //////////
Sat. ///////

For all its effectiveness, thought-stopping is reversible. You don't have to worry about taking irreversible steps away from your former love. What you need to do now is stop the pain. And that means you have to think about that person much, much less. If you want to reverse the process, you can do so by "stopping" the thought-stopping, and thinking positive, warm, erotic, tender thoughts about the person again.

•

Angelo, twenty-two. He quit his job rather than continue to see a woman at work who was no longer in love with him. There was no reasoning with Angelo. He did not care about reasons. Why should he? He was there. He knew her. He had several scenes ready to review at a moment's notice. "Remember the hot afternoon we had gone swimming in an icy cold pool in a roaring brook and she had . . ."

As is so often the case, the details are all specific, real, sometimes exquisitely pleasurable and, as you know, they can add up to a pain that's crippling. Or numbing, at least.

We had done thought-stopping for six days when the woman saw Angelo at the supermarket and later called him 21 and said she felt she had made a great mistake, and please could they meet and talk again. Angelo warily said yes, ceased thought-stopping and resumed the relationship. Later he said it was a little like falling in love all over again.

•

Like any exercise, thought-stopping has to be repeated. Doing it on purpose ten times a day would be a minimum number apart from all the times you think of your former love spontaneously throughout the day.

The first few days it does help to shout "STOP" out loud. So you need a quiet place of your own to practice. But after the first few days you can say "STOP" silently, or snap a rubber band that's wrapped around your wrist. Or you may find it helpful to dig a fingernail into your palm or clench your fists at the same time.

Thought-stopping takes time, repetition and effort. It may not work very well the first few times. And there may be setbacks. There will be times when thoughts of the person you loved will come back with great strength. Progress may not be smooth.

How quickly it works depends on how long you loved that person and how much. And how often you practice the technique. Every time you think of that person you should do thought-stopping. And you should set aside some ten minutes every day for practice.

Again, let me emphasize the importance of marking down, on a card, how many times you think of the person you want to stop loving. Continue to keep a record until you are down to four times a day.

Aaron, the nineteen-year-old whose list you read, found that he was thinking of the person he wanted to fall out of love with nearly fifty times a day. After practicing thought-stopping for two weeks, he was only thinking of her two or three times a day, leaving his mind free for new interests and new people.

One very beautiful fifty-year-old woman, who'd been left

by a man ten years younger, by her own count was thinking of her absent lover over a hundred times a day. She used the device of a rubber band around her wrist (after two days of shouting "STOP" out loud) and she found that in just over a week she was only thinking of him four times a day.

It may take you as little as a week to reach that point. It may stretch out for as long as a month. But you will find that you have at your fingertips the first, most powerful technique for falling out of love.

Exercises

Practice is essential. It helps make thought-stopping easy, and you need to have the technique at your fingertips, to use at will.

1. Ten times a day.
   a. Bring on (on purpose) a thought or image of your lover.
   b. The split second it begins to enter your mind, wipe it out by shouting, pounding, stamping your feet, digging a fingernail into your palm, snapping a rubber band that is wrapped around your wrist, and so on.
   c. Then replace it with a positive, pleasurable image from your list. This image should not in any way be associated with your former lover.
2. If the thought of your lover returns, drive it out again and replace it. This may require several repetitions before the thought will stay out for a period of time. You may need to drive it out as many as ten times.
3. Whenever, throughout the day, a thought or an image of your lover appears in your mind, wipe it out at the first split second by shouting, stamping your feet, digging a fingernail into your palm, snapping a rubber band that is around your wrist. Do not let that thought develop. Replace that thought with a positive, pleasurable thought that does not involve that person.

3

Silent Ridicule

Take a good look at yourself. And laugh. And take a good long look at the person you'd like to fall out of love with. And laugh again. I'm not joking, or being flip. Being able to laugh at yourself and your predicament is the single most important indicator of a healthy, positive outlook. No doubt the world would be intolerable if we were all healthy, positive people. On the other hand, there's certainly no danger of too much laughter. Laughter, or humor, is the best of all possible medicines for feeling depressed. It can give you the perspective and breathing room you need. The difficulty is that when you are feeling depressed, you don't laugh, particularly at yourself, your situation or at the person you love. What this chapter will do, then, is help you unlearn the pain you feel in response to that person by teaching you how to learn a little humor in a systematic way.

Thought-stopping helps you to think less about someone. Silent ridicule is a new technique that uses humor to help you think of him or her differently.

What, for example, if you have to see that person? What if you have to see him or her daily at work? Or what if you live in a small town or have the same friends and your paths cross inadvertently? And what if your friends talk about 25 that person, or you have to discuss the kids on the phone, talk about their school or their clothes and arrange for who will see the children on weekends and on vacation? And what if a child is a constant reminder of the other person because she looks or acts or talks so much like her father? Thought-stopping will reduce the number of times you think of someone, but it won't make the reality of someone's presence go away. And when you love someone who does not love you back, the pain that you feel when you see that person (all those old responses brought back, but wasted) is deeper than you can possibly explain. And all the will power in the world won't help very much.

Silent ridicule helps change your response to the person you love by changing the way you see that person. Instead of seeing them as you have in the past, you imagine them in an absurd, ridiculous, humorous scene.

You face something of a decision here. Thought-stopping is the first step. It helps reduce the pain. The question now is do you want to move further away from being in love with that person? Do you want to change the way you think and feel about that person? Because ultimately, whether it is the result of the passage of more time or your own purposeful action, falling out of love means thinking about that person, not only less often, but also in a different way.

Apart from the possibility of seeing, talking to, or hearing that person, there's another reason you might wish to change the way you think about him or her, and that's the pedestal. We all do it to some degree. We all tend to put a person up on a pedestal when we are in love. And from that angle, with the light shining in your eyes, it can be a little difficult to see the flaws. We make our lovers larger and more perfect than life. Petty but nasty habits like strewing dirty socks can be seen as endearing foibles ("He needs a little mothering"). Part of loving is exactly that, overlooking, ignoring, or forgiving small-scale irritants. However, you want to fall out of love. And it may be that that pedestal lifts that person right into the pure blue sky. Silent ridicule, as you will see, knocks the pedestal out from under their feet.

•

Malcolm, forty-seven-year-old advertising media buyer. Malcolm had lived with a woman for three years. She was, he said, a wonderful antidote to his tedious life at work. They planned imaginary trips together, mountain cabins they would build, farms they would farm. One day she left with no more than a short note saying that she was bored with him and leaving. Malcolm was devastated. He stayed home for a week, unable to work. He refused to believe she had really gone. He kept her clothes and her desk just as she had left them, even to the point of a book lying open at the page she had been reading. We did thought-stopping, but it was very difficult to get Malcolm to do silent ridicule. She was perfect as a person and the perfect person for him. She had a natural grace and dignity, he said, that made it impossible to imagine her as comic or absurd. And he did not want to think of her that way. After some discussion, I suggested that he should try thinking of her as a saint . . . a real plaster of paris madonna with pink and blue robes and a little shining halo around her head. He had to laugh.

Follow-up: Malcolm no longer keeps his museum to their past life. He changed jobs, and apartments. It was still some months before he formed another relationship.

•

Silent ridicule, imagining your former love in an absurd or comic context so that you can laugh at them and see their flaws, is as easy to do as thought-stopping. Suppose you want to fall out of love with your ex-husband. When you see him or talk to him or find that you are putting him on a pedestal, instantly imagine him in a ludicrous scene. That short-circuits your usual responses. Unlike thought-stop- 27 ping, it's not as easy to create appropriate situations. You may be willing to throw out the old photographs and letters and take his clothes down to the Salvation Army (which, by the way, is a good step toward no longer reinforcing your old responses to someone by getting rid of the old reminders of the past you shared). But the chances are you are somewhat reluctant to change your mind's pictures of him, even if you do suspect he enjoys rather special lighting effects in the theater of your mind.

So the discovery of the right scene for the one you want to fall out of love with is usually preceded by a difficult search. It is important to find the right scene, because once you do, it can work almost instantly. One striking example of silent ridicule's power to change longing and depression to objectivity was shown by a gifted student whose school-girl crush had developed into an obsession.

•

Marion, seventeen-year-old high-school senior. Marion was one of the brightest persons in her school. She had been virtually assured of acceptance into Harvard or Yale. Her English teacher was a young, handsome man who was an imaginative, enthusiastic teacher. Marion, who was not socially or sexually naïve, became infatuated with him. It may be that he encouraged the infatuation. In any case, when Marion came to me she was missing assignments, and she had become so involved in sexual fantasies in his classroom that she was unable to remember the content of the class. As she told me: "He has the most sensual mouth. I like to imagine tracing the outline of his lips with my tongue, drawing his lower lip into my mouth and sucking on it until it's a little tender or even sore, then drawing his wet mouth down to the nipple of my breast . . ."

Marion said she simply felt helpless in the force of what she felt for him. And that she was feeling deeply depressed about herself and her feelings. Changing teachers was one

28

obvious, but awkward, solution particularly since it was a small high school and she saw him repeatedly every day.

So while thought-stopping was a necessary, important first step, silent ridicule was even more important. In discussing Marion's teacher with her, we established that he was shorter than average height, an immaculate dresser, and vain about his appearance. After much discussion, I asked Marion to picture two things. First, her teacher wearing a homburg several sizes too large. And second, being hit in the face with a banana cream pie. She practiced the image at home and whenever she saw him.

Follow-up: Marion, now a sophomore in college, says that she'll always remain curious about him sexually, but that the too-big hat and pie in the face reduced him to the proper, realistic proportion and importance in her life. The one problem she'd had was giggling in the middle of class.

•

I know it can be hard to imagine the person you love in a silly situation. Therefore, as a therapist, I usually take an active role in helping people find an absurd situation or activity for the one they want to forget. You might find that a friend who knows the person you love can be particularly helpful since your friend's view of that person is apt to be more objective than yours. In addition, I'll give you some specific guidelines for designing an absurd scene that involves your former love. One important point is to be sure your scene is based on a foible or flaw or on an exaggeration of personality. You don't want your scene to evoke pity or the feeling that you ought to rescue them. If you feel that, don't struggle to suppress it; forget the scene and try another one. What you are after is a good laugh, not more sympathy for that person.

First, scan his or her environment. Where would they look most absurd? Where are they most anxious to make a good impression?

●

Jan, twenty-eight-year-old corporate secretary. Jan was in love with her boss, a member of the board of a large corporation. She found it both funny and helpful to picture him wearing diapers to a board meeting.

●

Henry, fifty-two-year-old actor. Henry was in love with a brilliant, totally captivating, mesmerizing art critic for a large metropolitan newspaper. He pictured her picking her nose at a gathering of people she most wanted to impress.

●

Randolph, thirty-four-year-old taxi driver. Randolph had lived for two years with someone he believed to be one of the most beautiful women in the world. When she returned to her wealthy husband, Randolph pictured her eating in a restaurant with her hair in curlers and wearing a housecoat and sneakers.

●

Franklin, forty-nine-year-old psychiatrist. Franklin had an affair with another psychiatrist, which she suddenly ended. She was always insisting on explanations for the subtlest shades of feeling. She was also very proper, wore gloves and a hat. Franklin pictured her standing on her head.

●

Next, microscopically examine that person for flaws. Exaggerate the flaw and/or use it out of context. Is that person vain, shy, aggressive, submissive, overly frank, slightly deceitful, sloppy, a fuss-budget, careless, overcautious, too thin, overweight, a health freak, conceited, self-deprecating? Does he pick his nose, teeth or toes? Does she . . . well, the list of possible human frailties is endless and often grubby. But it does help to fix on one, exaggerate it and imagine it in an absurd context.

●

30 *Pat, sixty-two-year-old suburban housewife.* Pat was in love with

the minister of her church. He was an eloquent speaker, particularly on subjects such as humility, grace and simplicity. He was, however, mightily dissatisfied with the house he was given by the church and said so in many ways. Pat imagined him living in a vast marble mansion, and complaining about it.

•

A little lunacy of the imagination helps too.

•

Cathy, forty-seven-year-old restaurant manager. She had been strung along for years by a local real-estate agent. She imagined him at a formal dinner party for all the local bigwigs. They were all elegantly dressed. He showed up wearing a Little Lord Fauntleroy costume with red velvet shorts, a lace collar, and holding a balloon. She liked to picture him in that outfit, dancing with the head of the school board, a large, somber woman in her seventies.

•

The scene doesn't have to be wildly exaggerated. Sometimes just a slight emphasis is all that's needed.

•

Ernestine, twenty-five years old. She was co-owner and manager of a restaurant with her husband. When he left her to live with another woman, they still saw each other for hours every day at the restaurant. He was the maître d' and Ernestine pictured him paying elaborate attention to a pretty woman at lunch so that the rest of the staff was snickering at him and the customers became impatient at the delay.

•

Sometimes it can be a very simple thing.

•

Karl, thirty-year-old policeman. He was married and in love with his best friend's wife. The two couples often spent weekends and holidays together, and saw each other at least 31 one evening a week. Karl was secretly in love with her but did not want to break up his marriage and lose his best friend. Her smile, he said, made him afraid he was going to make a fool of himself and spoil everything, so he pictured her with no teeth.

•

Silent ridicule is particularly useful in snatching the power from domineering authority figures.

•

Trish, twenty-two-year-old graduate student. Her father was one of the country's leading gynecologists, and was never pleased with anything his daughter did. She imagined him urinating in front of his patients in the waiting room.

•

Andrew, thirty-nine-year-old civil servant. Andrew was in love with his acting teacher, a large, powerful man, with a very strong personality. He told Andrew what to wear, where to be seen, what books to read, whom to admire, whom to disdain. Andrew pictured him acting the part of a detective in a staid Broadway play in the nude with a blue ribbon tied around his penis.

•

Once you do silent ridicule you may find it easier to laugh at yourself. And it's useful and sometimes hilarious to picture the person talking to you on the phone with Donald Duck's head or sucking on a baby bottle. It makes for a mad world, ducks' heads and baby bottles, but it's a fine way to stay sane. Humor chases anxiety the way dolphins bully sharks.

Exercises

1. Design a scene in which the person you love looks, acts and/or talks absurdly.
2. Practice alone, evoking the scene three to five times a day.
3. Then, whenever you see, talk to, or hear of that person, or start putting them on a pedestal, bring on the scene.

4

Positive Image Building and Congratulations

Being in love is the best known medicine for all kinds of negative feelings. People in love often get over fears and anxieties. Unfortunately, being in love and not being loved back has just the opposite effect. If you are in love, your existence, self-image and self-worth are defined by the person you love. However, being rejected may cause you to reject your existence and self-worth . . . to see those values as almost without value. Their rejection makes you depressed because depression can be caused by a lack of positive reinforcement (rewards in the form of praise, smiles, and encouragement, to use some of the more common terms). The feeling that you are rejected and not desired also takes away your energy. Things seem difficult, unmanageable and it simply becomes hard to cope. Then too, criticism from the one you love is particularly wounding. Criticism can make you doubt your own value and self-definition. ("Who are you, anyway?") And criticism can be manipulative. The person who criticizes assumes authority and power. All too often we are too quick to grant our critics authority, particularly when we love them. So being in love with someone and not being loved back, being rejected, and being criticized all change the way you

see yourself in specific, hurtful ways. The question, then, is how do you repair and improve that damaged picture of yourself?

It's an important question. The picture you have of yourself, however plain or fabulous, influences the way you treat yourself, the way you treat other people, and the way other people treat you. If you could take out that self-image, if it were possible to combine into one single photograph the kaleidoscope of mental snapshots, movies, portraits and scenes that make up your self-image, it might surprise you. If you could carefully and objectively examine your image of yourself, you might be surprised at how negative it is.

Most people's self-image goes way beyond the bounds of modesty and gets perilously close to self-contempt. Most people just don't see themselves in a very good light. Perhaps it's just human nature to focus on negatives. Perhaps it's because a large part of your self-image comes from other people: friends, parents, teachers, lovers, bosses, co-workers, whose criticism can be destructive of your self-esteem. Parents berate their kids for messy rooms and untied shoes. They tell their children they are too loud or too shy. It's simply the usual way of bringing up children: scold, correct, and chastise. Husbands tell their wives they shouldn't do this or that. And wives tell their husbands that they're fools for trying to do that or this. Perhaps it's just easier, as Hegel said, "to discover a deficiency in individuals, in states, and in Providence, than to see their real import and value." Whatever's behind this almost universal less-than-enthusiastic self-appraisal, it's been my experience that a negative self-image — being down on yourself — makes you unhappy, gets in the way of almost anything worthwhile you want to do, and is generally unrealistic. (It also gives some people the feeling of being a fraud. This is often true of people who are seen by others as "successful.")

In therapy, when a child has a negative self-image, I get his or her parents to give their child at least four compliments a day. And I try to get other people in the child's life (teachers, acquaintances) to do the same. But your world is not as simple as a child's. However, a child's story may serve as an illustration of an alternative to continuing depression. Do you remember *The Wizard of Oz?* The Tin Woodsman who had no heart, the Cowardly Lion who had no courage and the Scarecrow who had no brain? After years (maybe even centuries) of waiting around for a heart, courage and a brain, the three characters join Dorothy and go to meet the Wizard of Oz. When they start acting loving, brave and smart along the way, they find the heart, courage and brains they never knew they had. Which is the point. The way to acquire a positive self-image is to do positive things. It's much more efficient and rewarding to start doing active, assertive things than to spend your time looking for the reasons why you don't. The question is not "to be or not to be?" Do. The doing creates a positive feeling about yourself. It is precisely the opposite of waiting to feel positive before you do something positive. If the doing comes first, the feeling will follow.

Do what?

First, get a stack of ruled 8 by 5-inch index cards. They're available at every stationery store. Students and authors use them to keep an index of their notes. I find they're invaluable for keeping a record of progress. Of course, it's not absolutely essential that you write down the things I ask you to. But keeping a record lends your positive actions an authenticity, authority and permanence. It makes a graphic record of your progress. The discipline helps you keep up the exercise and it's not really very much extra effort.

Positives

Write down, every day, at least two positive things about yourself. Positive things can be a kind of general praise, "I'm smart," or they can be as concrete as putting the cap back on the toothpaste tube, letting a senior citizen have a seat on the bus, or replacing that burned-out light bulb you've been meaning to get around to for months. They can be big or small, from the past, present or future. You don't have to feel that it is one of the best things that you've ever done, merely that you can evaluate it as positive. It could be the way you look or how you related to someone . . . how you made someone feel welcome, happy or just plain good. It can be something you did or the way you did it ("I did a good job of bolting on that tire, those bolts are really secure"). It can be something you wear ("I like the way this shirt looks on me"), or something you enjoy ("This is a game I could really get into"), or ("a terrific movie").

Assertiveness can be very useful to you now. It inhibits anxiety and tends to give you a more positive picture of yourself. As you act stronger, you see that you are stronger. Moreover, you change your environment for the better. As people see you act more assertively, they are less apt to treat you as a second-rate person and more likely to respect you. And, in being assertive, you stand a better chance of getting what you want.

So now the point is not only to praise yourself but to encourage yourself to start moving toward positive actions that have some degree of assertiveness. ("I returned that faulty gizmo to the store." "Expressed my opinion on the banks to Walter.") Don't give yourself a halfhearted, left-handed compliment. ("Well, I did finish it, but I had to." "It wasn't my best.") Be generous. Praise yourself. And praise yourself in writing for six weeks. Apart from feeling better about yourself, another benefit of this exercise is that you'll 37 grow stronger and less dependent on the praise of others, because you can now praise yourself and evaluate yourself in a positive way. Here are three examples of positive cards.

Forty-two-year-old executive

Mon.   Drove kids to school. Wore best tie.

Tues.   Had idea for new product; doormats with rude sayings. Saw a good movie.

Wed.   Ran good meeting with salespeople. Drew picture of an elephant that looks like an elephant.

Thurs.   Stayed home in evening and relaxed. Enjoyed reading Travis McGee mystery.

Fri.   Did exercises in the morning. Walked faster than usual.

Sat.   Took Frankie to the store. Did not buy him candy.

Sun.   Had dinner with the kids. Read Jonathan a Pat Hutchins story.

Mon.   Walked to train station. Had salad for lunch.

Tues.   Really love the kids. Had salad for lunch.

Wed.   Got up and went to work (great effort). Thought positively about my future (first time in months).

Twenty-eight-year-old mother

Wed.   Exercise class. Did three loads of wash. Prepared address list for PTA.

Thurs.   Exercise class. Went to PTA meeting.

Fri.   Washed wall for painting. Errands. Prepared dinner.

Sun.   Enjoyed dinner with Joel. Coffee with Barb.

Mon.   Tired, but handled two sick kids. Did nothing for twenty minutes but soak in tub.

Twenty-four-year-old postal worker

38   Tues.   Said "no" to Ned. Got new shoes.

Wed. Cleaned bathroom. Worked out the house thing with Bob.

Thurs. Decisiveness about change. Response to Willie saying he was leaving.

Fri. Pushing to get together with the Williamses . . . Took kids to movie and dinner.

Sat. Solved kids' fight in morning. Judy's lunch note.

Sun. Stayed awake in church. Cooked excellent dinner.

Mon. Showed new person how to do job. Helped new person.

Tues. Started gardening book. Bought tomato seeds.

Thought-stopping

Use thought-stopping on self-critical thinking and with depressing thoughts. There are times when self-criticism may be useful tonic. But not now. The first instant you begin to sense a self-critical thought, kill it. Shout "STOP" to yourself and cut off that destructive thought before it has a chance to take root. Replace it with one of your pleasurable scenes. Or, it's even better if you can switch to a self-assertive thought ("This is me gently but firmly refusing an offer of Danish pastry and coffee"). Switching to a self-assertive thought isn't necessary, just a bonus if you can do it.

Dwelling on self-critical thoughts is not productive. Such a negative approach leads you to feel worse, less able to cope and less able to recognize your own self-worth. There are therapists who say that pain produces insight. I disagree. Tearing yourself apart is not useful. Pain produces more pain. When you think a depressing thought, you oppress yourself. It can be very hard to break that depressing cycle. When a man in my office is in a depression, full of negative thoughts about himself, I tell him that for the next fifteen minutes I will not allow him to say anything negative   39 about himself. And I cut him off if he does. You should do the same. Cut off self-critical thoughts the first microsecond they appear.

Be Assertive

Being assertive improves your self-image. Because assertiveness competes with anxiety. As Dr. Wolpe (a pioneer in assertive training) points out, assertive behavior lessens inhibitions in an exercise of self. In other words, acting assertively makes it possible to feel positive emotions more strongly. And the stronger you feel, the more you reduce your inhibitions and anxiety. The more you learn to control situations, the less situations control you. (There are any number of books on assertive behavior; one of the best is *Your Perfect Right* by Robert Alberti and Michael Emmons, and *When I Say No, I Feel Guilty* by Manuel Smith is useful for the techniques of "fogging" and "broken record.") The focus here is on improving your self-image, so I'll simply give you a brief introduction to assertive behavior and then concentrate on how you can use assertiveness to see yourself more positively.

Assertiveness is the ability and the emotional freedom to express opinions and feelings openly, with confidence and strength. Assertiveness is standing up for yourself, and not letting anybody take advantage of you. It shares some obvious qualities with aggressiveness, but unlike aggressiveness, you are not out to hurt, manipulate or take advantage of anyone. One often quoted passage from the Talmud says, "If I am not for myself, who will be for me?" The much less quoted second half of that says, "But if I am only for myself, what am I?" Dr. Alan Goldstein, a leading behavior therapist at Temple University Medical School, describes assertiveness as "the ability to bring about the most beneficial

40

result in a situation for oneself," with the added proviso of not deliberately causing harm to others.

Like other emotions and behaviors, assertiveness is learned. As you learn assertiveness step by step, becoming stronger and less anxious in social situations, your self-image will improve in a direct step-by-step parallel. So you begin in a small way with easy things first. Ask someone you know for a small favor, or express an opinion about the weather ("I think it's warm enough"). As commonplace and as ordinary as the opinion may be, it is, for some, an essential first trial step. The point is to make it easy on yourself so that you know you will succeed. Happily, assertiveness also improves the way people think of you. Because if you are assertive, instead of timid or aggressive, if you are self-confident, instead of wishy-washy, you change your environment as people tend to respond to you more positively. People take advantage of you less and value you more.

Changing your self-image means learning to think more positively about yourself. The negative images you have of yourself may be strong or weak. In either case, they won't be changed by deciding to change them. Rationality doesn't help much. You can't resolve to feel better about yourself in the morning any more than you could resolve to stop thinking about someone and thereupon magically stop or resolve to cheer up when you're blue. Changing your self-image takes exercise and practice. Again, you have to re-learn on an emotional level. Because the facts don't, won't and can't change. What you can change is the emotional light in which you see yourself.

I have a whole catalogue of assertiveness exercises for you to browse through. I say browse, because you may not want or need to do them all. But in looking at yourself and observing how you see yourself (weak, strong, decisive, wishy-washy, amusing, boring, intelligent, dumb, honest, 41 crafty, important, insignificant, bold, shy, positive, negative), you may find that several of these exercises are not only useful, but necessary. For each assignment that you choose to do, make out an 8 by 5-inch card with the title of the assignment at the top and list the days of the week down the left-hand side so that you can record your experience and progress. Here's an example of how a card might look for the exercise I call opinions:

Opinions

Mon.   Told Harry I like his old suit. Talked with Sue about improving the park.

Tues. Told Grant I think he has a great sense of humor. Told Peggy she's beautiful.

Wed.   Said I'm bored with the same tired menu to cafeteria manager.

Thurs. Told Matty I think of that crook in the Senate. Told Matty he has a lovely smile.

Fri.   Said it'd be nice if we all had lunch together. Said I get bored with beautiful weather.

Sat.   Said Matty was showing off. Said Matty should show off more frequently.

Sun.   I hate figs. I think a bicycle's a terrific idea.

Mon.   It'd be great to be a clown (to Harry). I like reading trash (to Peggy).

Tues. I will always hate stewed figs. Diets are dopey; eat less (both to cafeteria manager).

Should any exercise cause you any anxiety, tension or discomfort, don't do it. You don't want to put yourself in a losing situation or cause yourself more pain. Always make sure that the positive emotion (assertiveness, confidence) wins and the anxiety loses so that you feel more positive and less anxious. If you still want to do the exercise, try it out on the cat or dog, or silently in your own mind. And then, once you can imagine it and/or carry it out without discomfort, you can go on to try it out in a more challenging situation. On the other hand, if you feel you are already beyond an exercise, good. Skip it. What you should do is build yourself up by easy steps until you can handle much more threatening or negative situations than you could before.

Assertive Assignments

1. COMPLIMENTS (for three weeks or until it is easy). Accept all compliments without downgrading yourself.
   Example: Instead of replying, "Oh, I got it five years ago as a bargain," say, "I'm really glad you like it."
   Example: Instead of replying, "Anybody could have done it," say, "I'm happy you noticed."
   Make a note of each compliment and write down your response. As a corollary, start noticing things and people in your environment that you can compliment. Giving someone a compliment is an expressive thing to do, and it helps you bring yourself out of a depressed, nonactive state.

2. OPINIONS (for three weeks or until it is easy). Express two opinions a day. Start with nonthreatening subjects and express them to nonthreatening people (or even objects), gradually increasing the degree of controversy of the subjects and by degrees expressing yourself to more threatening people. Your opinions can be positive or negative, as long as they are yours.
   Important: You don't have to say how things make you feel, merely what you think.
   Example: To a friend, "I think we should have lunch with Charles."

43

Example: To the bedroom wall, "I think it's too cold to go outside."

Example: To a friend, "Frankly I thought that show was sensational."

Example: To your brother, "I think it's time you burned that hairpiece."

Write down the opinions you express on a card.

3. *I* (for one week or until it is easy). Begin five sentences a day with the word "I." Instead of saying, "It's warm in here," say, "I am warm in here."

4. FEELING FEELINGS (for three weeks). Eight times throughout the day, stop and check out the feeling that you have at that moment. Every time you have a feeling such as feeling glad, excited, happy, relaxed, calm, funny, grateful, confident, and so on, write it down. Begin with at least two a day.

5. EXPRESSING FEELINGS (from now on). When you feel comfortable writing down feelings, express one or two feelings a day to one or two people. Begin with easy feelings with friends.

Example: "I'm really glad you called. It's good to hear your voice."

Example: "Ha, ha, ha, ha, ha, ha, ha, ha, ha, ha, ha."

Example: "I feel a little uncomfortable with all these people around."

Work up to stronger feelings with people who are in some ways difficult to express feelings to.

Example: "I feel vulnerable and exposed when you say things like that."

Example: "I feel guilty and there's no reason why I should feel guilty."

Example: "This suit makes me feel elegant."

Example: "I want you all to know I'm very proud of this dinner."

44

Always make it easy on yourself. Don't make yourself anxious. Don't do anything that makes you uncomfortable. Make sure assertiveness wins over anxiety.

6. MODELING (whenever you try any of the exercises 4–11 and whenever you feel you need extra confidence). Get an image in your mind of someone you think of as very self-confident. Keep that individual in mind as you try to act the way they might act. Think of and use the words they would use, their tone of voice, eye contact, posture and self-confidence.

7. SAY NO (twice a week). If you never or rarely say "no," practice saying "no" at least twice a week when someone asks you to do something you don't want to do. However, if it makes you feel tense, begin by just thinking about saying "no." In either case, write down on a card all the times you think or say "no."

8. A FAVOR (once a week). If you are not used to asking for a favor, ask. Begin with a very small favor from someone you know well.

Adventures

You deserve to be treated considerately. To earn consideration you have to ask for it. And you will have to practice assertive behavior in order to learn to ask. These exercises are like the basic exercises you do when you learn to play tennis or softball. They stretch and develop new emotional muscles, reduce your anxiety and help you toward a better self-image.

9. BUY SOMETHING. And return it. For getting things your way.

10. QUIET TABLE. Go into a restaurant and insist, firmly but nicely, on a quiet table. (There are times, of course, 45

when this is not practical.) Other examples might be asking the cab driver to drive more slowly or more quickly, asking the bus driver to let you know when you reach your stop, asking for special commemorative stamps at the post office.

11. SIMPLE FARE. Go into a very fancy restaurant and order a very simple meal, "Just a salad, please" or "Just the soup, please." The "beautiful people" do it all the time. It's one way some of them stay slim.

12. TEACH. Teach someone to read, dance, or exercise, or how to saw a straight line. This is one of the best exercises of all. It gives you the emotional reward that comes with doing something worthwhile and with giving something to someone else. And, of course, there is the extra bonus of realizing that you have something worthwhile to give.

13. LEARN. The world is full of things to learn. How to grow your own, how to dance, how to make something, how to fix something else, how directors make movies, how movie stars make love, what Sophocles said about knowledge, what Joan of Arc was really like. Learning is more than a distraction. It can give you a new skill, a new purpose. It can exercise and strengthen your mind. It can introduce you to a whole new realm of possibilities and people.

14. REHEARSAL (then *try it out*). With a friend or by yourself act out the following situations:

A. You are in line. Someone cuts in front of you. You ask him/her to go to the end of the line. You tell him/her to go to the end of the line. He or she goes to the end of the line.

B. In a restaurant the steak is overdone. Ask the waiter, quietly but firmly, to take it back.

C. At a fancy beach resort, a lifeguard tells you to leave

because this is a private beach. Tell the lifeguard the law in the town says there is no such thing as a private beach.

Self-Indulgence

Self-indulgence is a way of giving yourself positive reinforcement. Here are a few suggestions. You may well think of other, better ones. Being good to yourself isn't a luxury, it's a pleasure. And for positive reinforcement, a necessity.

15. BED. Stay in bed an extra three minutes in the morning.

16. LOTION. Enjoy the sensation of putting on hand lotion slowly.

17. IF YOU CAN'T THINK OF ANYTHING GOOD TO DO FOR YOURSELF. Think of something good to do for a friend or just call an old friend or do something good for your house or apartment.

18. CANDY (once a month). Find three superb chocolates and eat them very slowly.

19. CATS. Watch how a cat seeks pleasure in each moment. Notice how it seeks out the most comfortable spot in the room. And how it stretches. And how it climbs on you when it wants to be petted. Spend ten minutes like a cat.

20. ONE DAY (once a month). Spend one day as if it were your only day. Just today. What would you like to do?

21. EXERCISE. Of course you should. It's easiest if you go to an exercise, dance or yoga class. But you can also do sit-ups, touch your toes and jog. Lots of books are available. It makes your body stronger and your mind function better.

47

22. BUBBLE BATH. Soak.

The hardest part of any of the foregoing twenty-two things to do is doing them. In themselves they are, by and large, easy enough. You may well agree that some would, or at least could, actually improve your life.

If you think you could use an added push, you might ask someone you know to be an "enabler." Enabling is an idea I first heard about from a group of church women in Washington who wanted to be more active and effective in helping each other and their children. An enabler is something like a friendly schoolmaster who makes sure you do your lessons. Here's how it works. Tell your friend what you want to do and how you plan to do it. You then report to your enabler regularly. Your enabler both encourages you and holds you accountable for keeping to your schedule. For example, if you set out to express two opinions a day, or start five sentences a day with "I" or jog two miles a day, you report to your enabler daily what you have achieved. Having to be accountable to someone else and having the encouragement and support of another person can give you more discipline and motivation than you might have on your own.

Congratulations

This last suggestion is a treat, a small useful technique that behavior therapists call positive reinforcement.

B. F. Skinner originated the technique with specific rewards. And Joseph Cautela designed a variation, called covert reinforcement, to include the intangible, but real rewards of silent praise and pleasures.

Congratulations is a way to strengthen your progress by rewarding yourself for taking constructive steps. And it

48 helps you recognize your ability to make a positive change.

For the more you focus on a behavior, the more likely it is for that behavior to recur. In fact, any attention we give to specific behavior tends to strengthen that behavior and increase its frequency. For example, if you praise a child's one glimmer of good table manners, you are apt to see an overall improvement in the child as a dinner companion. And conversely, scolding a child for messy table habits is apt to prolong the mess. After all, we all like attention.

Here is how you use congratulations for falling out of love. Suppose you've been thinking about telephoning your former love, or taking out a photograph of the two of you together and looking at it. And instead, you turn away from the phone or close the dresser drawer where the pictures are kept. Closing the drawer and turning away from the phone are both positive actions that, like thought-stopping, help extinguish thoughts about that person. For taking that positive step, congratulate yourself and give yourself a small reward. You want to encourage and reinforce that kind of behavior. So give yourself a record, a new paperback, take a leisurely shower or soak in a bubble bath, call a friend, take a walk in an interesting place, buy yourself a snack, or take a three-minute vacation from the world by closing your eyes and picturing peaceful, passing clouds in a blue sky. After all, you've earned a reward.

The last reward is a mini-vacation. Suppose you are walking down a street and you are tempted to walk past the place where your former lover lives, "just to see if she is there." And you don't, you don't turn down that street. Or suppose you take the positive, assertive action of asking your friends not to mention the person you want to fall out of love with during the evening. In either case, or in any other case, you can reward yourself on the spot for free by simply picturing a beautiful place you'd like to be, a beach, a sports car, an ancient oak-paneled library of rare books, the fifty-yard line of the Super Bowl. These pleasurable thoughts are free and make a good reward for positive ac- 49 tions. If you have difficulty picturing a new pleasurable scene that does not include your former love, you might recall one of your favorites from your thought-stopping list.

So as you notice you're thinking about your former love less, and when you take a positive step away from that person, reward yourself with congratulations.

5

Jealousy

"It's like being possessed," said one man. "I was totally controlled by it. I would seriously consider whether I should kill myself or the person I loved or my rival or all three of us." Another man said that the only other time he'd had so much pain (and fear) was during heart surgery. A woman told me, "I hate it. I hate it. I can't get rid of it."

In the range of human emotions, jealousy strikes a vicious, primal claim. It destroys marriages, love affairs and friendships. Some parents feel jealous when a child is born. Cain, son of Adam in the Bible, slew his brother out of jealousy. Medea killed her own children and Othello killed his bride, Desdemona, out of jealousy. Jealousy demands immediate, total attention, blocking all other emotions and considerations. Almost everyone has suffered from it. And you know it's a parasite that feeds on love. You know it makes you selfish, possessive, anxious and repulsive — full of hate, anger and suspicion. You know it makes you an ugly pawn to its demands. And you know that just feeling the emotion is a dead-end trap that damages what you want most. You know all that. But once you start feeling jealous, there doesn't seem to be much you can do about it. After centuries of talking and writing about jealousy, the prevailing theory seems to be that the way you overcome jealousy is by an act of will. I strongly disagree. I don't think you 51 can will jealousy away. It has to be emotionally unlearned.

Jealousy is a negative emotion that keeps you from falling out of love, while at the same time it keeps you from feeling love. It keeps you emotionally bound to and emotionally dependent on the person you love. To fall out of love you have to break the emotional involvement that jealousy demands.

As you have seen, thought-stopping and silent ridicule help you stop thinking about that person and change the way you think about them. And positive image building gives you a more positive picture of yourself. But if you are jealous, you will need more help. Why, for example, in the face of its repulsiveness and in the knowledge of its unlimited capacity for destroying a loving relationship do we allow jealousy to exist in our minds? At least part of the answer is that jealousy is irrational. For all its agility and speed in finding apparently rational reasons, excuses and subterfuges, jealousy has its roots deep in the emotions. Possibly you first learned jealousy when you were an infant in your crib. Possibly before you could walk or talk, another person walked into the room and your mother stopped playing with you. Possibly you felt deprived of your mother's love, anxious that you might never get it back, and fearful of the power of the other person who could so easily lure your mother away from you. Possibly that person was your father.

Possibly. But for whatever reason you first learned jealousy, knowing that reason is unlikely to help. Rational explanations of former emotions can never be certain and are beside the point. To unlearn jealousy, you must unlearn on that same emotional level. Thought-stopping applied to jealousy is helpful in emotionally unlearning jealousy. (The first instant you begin to feel a jealous thought, you shout "STOP" to yourself and replace the jealous thought with a pleasurable, positive thought that does not involve the person in the jealous thought.) But usually, along with

52

thought-stopping, I use another technique I call graduated calming. (It's based on Dr. Joseph Wolpe's method of calming, reducing and extinguishing anxieties, which is technically called desensitization.)

As Dr. Wolpe points out in his introduction, one of the most important discoveries of behavior therapy is that an anxiety like jealousy can be reduced or extinguished if, while you are deeply relaxed, you can imagine a scene or an experience that usually causes anxiety. Because deep relaxation inhibits anxiety.

For many years, jealousy was thought to be an inevitable force of nature. Traditional therapy gives one insights, but as I have suggested, the insights do not make you feel less jealous. Graduated calming, on the other hand, does make you feel less jealous. I have been teaching the technique for overcoming jealousy for almost four years and it works. The technique is best handled by a therapist because a therapist can evaluate your emotional history and, based on that, make an analysis of your behavior to determine the events and emotions for graduated calming. And, of course, a behavior therapist would guide and assist the whole graduated calming process. Still, I want to spend a little extra time giving you a working knowledge of graduated calming because I believe it can be a great help to you in dealing with jealousy even without a therapist. There are no harmful side effects from graduated calming, and you might find it very helpful. At the very least, learning graduated calming will give you a new way to relax, an objective look at your jealous feelings, and an inside view of how behavior therapy works.

Graduated calming is relearning on a neurological and emotional level. It changes your thoughts, feelings, perceptions, sensations and, most important, your anxiety levels. Graduated calming takes you slowly, step by step, up what behavior therapists call an anxiety (or any other negative emotion) hierarchy, as first described by Dr. Wolpe. In this chapter, the negative emotion that will be reduced is jealousy. You begin with deep muscle relaxation, imagine a situation that causes you some jealousy, and then return to deep relaxation.

Learning graduated calming is a three-step process, beginning with learning deep muscle relaxation, followed by establishing your own jealousy hierarchy, followed by learning the graduated calming process.

Deep Muscle Relaxation

The old adage, "Lie down, and you will feel better," has more than a grain of truth in it. Relaxation combats anxiety. There is a direct relationship between the degree of muscle relaxation and the degree of positive emotional change away from anxiety. So I am going to teach you how to relax far beyond your usual degree of relaxation. With practice you'll be able to relax deeply at will, and diminish your anxiety.

Before going through the complete deep muscle relaxation process, I'd like to give you an idea of the principle involved. I want you right now to make a fist, and tighten all the muscles in your right arm. Make the muscles as tight and as hard as you can so that your arm is as rigid as you can make it. Notice all the sensations in your arm and concentrate on the muscle tension in your biceps. Now I want you to let go gradually, relax your arm slowly, and notice how that "letting go" is an activity itself. It is the uncontracting of your muscles. Keep on letting go until your arm feels totally relaxed. I say "feels" totally relaxed because, although most of the muscle fibers in your arm feel relaxed, some of the muscles will still be contracted. So keep on letting go. Try to continue that letting go activity beyond the point of simple relaxation and deeply relax all the muscles in your arm. Notice the feeling in your arm.

54

Now clench your fist again and make your whole arm as rigid as iron. Make it as tight as you possibly can and become aware of what your arm feels like. Keep on being aware of that feeling as you begin to relax. See if you can picture the muscles in your arm as you totally relax your arm. Let your arm relax even more. If you concentrate all of your attention on your arm, you will find some few muscle fibers are still tense. It is the relaxation of those additional fibers that will bring about deep relaxation. So repeat the process of slowly tightening and relaxing your arm, being aware of the muscles in your arm and observing them as they relax, and when you feel your arm completely relaxed, see if you can go beyond that furthest point and relax still further. Try to go beyond what seems to be the furthest point.

That's a fair example of deep muscle relaxation, a systematic way of driving out tension by letting your mind become aware of and relaxing each part of your body in turn by concentrating on that part of your body, feeling any muscles that might be tense and letting them go.

Deep muscle relaxation requires that you become physically passive. Yet you remain an alert observer and reporter of your own body's degree of relaxation.

Most people can't fully relax on their first try. Deep relaxation has to be learned, and it does take practice. So while fifteen or twenty minutes of relaxation may, at first, just relax your forearm, eventually you'll be able to relax your whole body in a minute or two. On the other hand, you might just be one of those lucky people who, on their very first attempt at deep relaxation, experience deepening and extending relaxation radiating throughout their body and feel general effects such as calmness, sleepiness or warmth. The effect that you want to achieve is a peaceful and calm state where you feel no tension, no anxiety, no worries, no negative emotions whatsoever.

If you have access to a tape recorder, you might like to 55

record the next section in an easy, relaxed voice. And then whenever you want to practice deep muscle relaxation listen to the tape. You'll find it's a great help because, with the tape recorder giving you instructions, your mind will be free to follow and find the muscles that need relaxing.

Find a comfortable, quiet place where you know you won't be disturbed. Now make yourself comfortable by lying down or stretching out on a sofa or sitting back in an easy chair. Then, with your arms at your sides and your legs straight out with your feet slightly apart, relax.

Erase the thoughts of the things that happened today. Make your mind a perfect blank. Let go of all your worries and hopes and fears . . . feel your mind just float free in space. Now be aware of your left leg. Picture the muscles and bones in your left leg. Lift your left leg six inches off the floor and tighten all the muscles in your left leg . . . tighter and tighter until it is rigid. Now all at once, let go of all the muscles in your left leg and let it drop. Roll it slowly from side to side a couple of times to be sure all the muscles are completely relaxed. Just let it lie there, totally relaxed. Now bring your mind's awareness to your right leg. Picture the muscles and bones inside. Lift the leg six inches off the floor, tighten all your right leg muscles until they are rigid, keep your leg rigid for a couple of moments, then drop it, roll it from side to side, completely relaxed, and forget it.

Now bring your mind to your left arm. Concentrate on the muscles and bones in your left arm. Lift it six inches in the air and tighten all the muscles as hard as you can. Tighten harder. Then let the arm drop. Roll it from side to side a couple of times to make sure it is completely relaxed, and then forget it. Now bring your mind to your right arm. Concentrate on the muscles and bones of your right arm. Lift it six inches and tighten all the muscles as hard as you can. Tighten harder. Then let the arm drop. Roll it from side to side a couple of times to make sure your right arm is completely relaxed, and then forget it.

Now tighten your buttocks. Squeeze as hard as you can, hold it, tighter, now let go and relax. Inhale so that your stomach pushes out as far as it will go. Squeeze in another breath so that it expands out farther. Hold it. Now exhale . . . let it go all at once and forget it. Relax.

Bring your awareness to your chest and shoulders. Lift your shoulders up and with your arms completely relaxed, tighten your shoulder and chest muscles as if you were trying to touch your shoulders in front of you. Tighter. Now let your shoulders drop. Relax.

Now picture all the muscles in your neck and tighten them. Tighten them so hard the cords in your neck stand out. Tighter. Let go all at once. Relax. Roll your head gently from side to side to be sure all the neck muscles are relaxed.

Now squeeze your face muscles as if you were trying to bring all of the features of your face to one point around your nose. Make your face as tight and pursed as if it were becoming a prune. Now let go.

Take a deep breath and hold it. Open your eyes and your mouth as wide as you can. Stick your tongue out as far as it will go. Open your eyes and your mouth wider so you can feel your face stretch. Stick out your tongue farther. Now all at once, let out your breath and relax your face. Relax.

Your body should be completely relaxed. Let your mind cruise down to your left and your right legs, your left arm and your right arm, your stomach, buttocks, shoulders, chest, neck, and face in turn to be sure that all the muscles in your body are peaceful and relaxed. Search out any tension that may still remain in any muscle, and let go of that muscle. Let it relax still further. Allow yourself enough time to go slowly over your body, and ease any tension that may still remain. You might feel drowsy or warm or a kind 57 of pleasant tingling. Feel how good it feels to be calm and relaxed.

You can become twice as relaxed as you are merely by taking in a really deep breath and slowly exhaling. With your eyes closed (so that you become less aware of objects and movements around you and can thus prevent any surface tensions from developing), breathe in deeply and feel yourself becoming heavier. Take in a long, deep breath and let it out very slowly. Feel how heavy and relaxed you have become. Some people find they can deepen their relaxation further by mentally reviewing the parts of their bodies and saying to themselves, "My foot [or calf or thigh or whatever] is limp and warm and heavy." This should be done slowly, repeating each statement once or twice so your body has time to respond to your instructions.

In a state of perfect relaxation you should feel unwilling to move a single muscle in your body. Think about the effort that would be required to raise your right arm. As you think about raising your right arm, see if you can notice any tensions that might have crept into your shoulder and your arm.

Now you decide not to lift the arm but to continue relaxing. Observe the relief and the disappearance of the tension.

Just carry on relaxing like that. When you wish to get up, count backward from four to one. You should then feel fine and refreshed, wide awake and calm.

So that is deep muscle relaxation. Practice deep muscle relaxation twice a day (in bed at night before going to sleep is a good time, because it will also help you get to sleep) until you can do it easily. After you've thoroughly mastered the technique, you won't need to do the tensing exercises I've described.

Jealousy Hierarchy

As you are acquiring a facility for deep muscle relaxation, you should also take some extra time out from your day to list the things that make you feel jealous. After you list them, you can rate them according to the amount of jealousy each one of those things (people, places or situations) makes you feel.

A jealousy hierarchy is simply a list, in ascending order of intensity, of the things that make you jealous, on a scale of zero to one hundred. Zero would be total calm and relaxation as in deep muscle relaxation. And one hundred would be the most jealousy you could possibly feel.

Quite apart from graduated calming, having a specific list of your own jealousies in order of intensity has two other benefits. First, quantifying jealousy helps reduce it. The fact that a jealous thought is brought out into the open and put into an order helps to bring order to the chaos of your anxiety. And, second, it is more meaningful to be able to say to yourself (or to your therapist), "I feel at sixty," as opposed to the usual vague description, "I feel awful."

Here's what the scale means in terms of what you feel.

0	Total relaxation. No jealousy. No negative thoughts whatsoever.
10, 20	Mild, jealous feeling . . . barely noticeable.
30, 40, 50	Moderate jealousy. Definitely feeling uneasy. You might feel butterflies in your stomach or the start of a tension headache.
60, 70	High jealousy. You can feel your heart pounding, head/stomach ache. Real distress.
80, 90	Intense, severe jealousy approaching rage or panic. Something you want to avoid at all costs.

59

100   Panic. The most jealousy you can possibly imagine.

Most people find that a pleasant, relaxing scene that does not involve their former love is useful in achieving zero on the relaxation scale and in returning back to zero when a thought causes them to feel some jealousy. However, it doesn't have to be a "scene" at all. It could be as simple as picturing clouds in the sky, or the ocean. Just as long as it is peaceful and bland. Getting down to zero is a problem if your usual state of mind is at the near frenzy of seventy or eighty on the scale. One man who habitually felt extremely tense and anxious (he was living at seventy, we later decided) got down to zero in his first session. But that is exceptional. You may find that deep relaxation takes much more practice and time before you can get down to a completely relaxed state of mind and body. A warm bath, music or reading a dull book beforehand can be helpful. Making your mind a complete blank, practicing driving out all thoughts beforehand, is another useful exercise.

Next, the thoughts or situations in your own hierarchy don't require a vivid imagination, even though you may be blessed with one. What you will need is to be a good reporter of your own reactions. Whenever you feel jealous, you should take note of what it is that makes you feel jealous and you should write that down. You should also assign it a number on your hierarchy scale according to the amount of jealousy it inspires (for example, "She's talking to him about her vacation — forty").

Finally, make a separate check on yourself throughout the day to see where you are on the scale so that you learn to recognize and rate your feelings. This not only helps to fill out your hierarchy list, but helps you learn to recognize and objectify your negative feelings.

As in the making of your thought-stopping list, there is no such thing as a "good" list or a "bad" one, an "average" list or an "abnormal" list. We are all so different that the thought of a former lover talking to a good friend may leave some of us at zero and others at one hundred. So while it's difficult for me to guess what you should put at the top or the bottom of your jealousy hierarchy, you may find some examples helpful.

•

Melissa, forty-four years old, married twenty-three years to a stockbroker. She'd had, what seemed to many of her friends, a wonderful marriage. Four happy, healthy, intelligent kids, and a big, warm, beautiful home. Both she and her husband were dynamic, bright, sensitive people. Then her husband announced that he was in love with a younger woman, a lawyer whom he'd met at his office. He said he was leaving Melissa.

Melissa had built her whole life around him. It seemed incredible to her, totally unfair, that he could just walk out. Perhaps, she felt, he had never really been in love with her. Perhaps their life together had been a lie. But she clung to her old model of a happy marriage she had worked so hard to achieve. And, not surprisingly, she felt intensely jealous over his new partner. Particularly galling were his hints of newfound sexual pleasure and intimacy. Why had she been denied that? What had she done wrong, or not known? Her suffering was intense and aggravated by living in a small community in the Midwest where "everyone knew."

We did thought-stopping, which greatly diminished the number of times she thought about her husband. But her image of herself on a high summer noon, swimming nude in the surf of the Big Sur, was not enough to stop her intense feelings of jealousy. I taught Melissa deep muscle relaxation and together we made the following jealousy hierarchy.

•

Melissa's Jealousy Hierarchy

0   Seeing and hearing the wave-lap of the sea on the pilings of a wharf in a fishing village.

20   Her rival's friendship with her own children.

35   Her rival relating to and being liked by her husband's parents.

50   Seeing them together.

65   Seeing them happy together.

70   Imagining them talking about her.

80   Their experimenting and enjoying each other sexually.

100   Losing her husband to her rival forever.

Graduated calming did not effect a magic cure for Melissa. In her own eyes and in the eyes of her friends, she had suffered both a defeat and an emotional loss. All the habits, all the responses, all the feelings of twenty-three years of her life were suddenly useless or called into question or, from her point of view, pointless. On the other hand, she became alert to her own brand-new possibilities. Thought-stopping radically decreased the time she spent thinking about her husband. Silent ridicule, picturing him with a bowl of oatmeal overturned on his head, made him less of an infallible authority figure. Positive image building helped Melissa out of feeling physically and intellectually inadequate and conscious of her own considerable gifts. And graduated calming helped her stop brooding about her "rival" and begin to take steps to make her own new life. Her own new life, by the way, has a great deal to be said for it. With her children nearly grown up, in or graduated from college, she moved to a nearby city and went to work for a TV station. Through her own energy, curiosity and ability she became the producer of a weekly hour-long news show, an outlet unavailable to her inside the confines of her picture of an ideal marriage. She has many new friends and as much male companionship as she likes but she is not anxious, understandably, to enter into a new, long-term relationship.

•

Melissa sent a young man from the TV station to me. Of all the people that I have met, he was the one who was most afflicted by jealousy.

•

Jesse, forty-nine-year-old TV director. By any measure you would have to describe Jesse as unique. He had that single-mindedness bordering on fanaticism that makes great work possible in the face of distractions or indifference. Unfortunately, that single-mindedness also applied to jealousy. It was a great passion with him. He would hear of good friends having dinner and not inviting him and feel rejected, although he knew he was much too busy to have joined them. A lover (he was bisexual and had several lovers) would be late for a date and Jesse would imagine him (or her) in scenes of animal passion with someone else and he would be physically paralyzed, unable to work for two days. Seeing a former lover having a good time with other people would cause him great anxiety and pain. Although he had won many awards and his work had been discussed, analyzed and praised in books, television and newspapers, the publication of a book on TV drama that did not have a section devoted to him caused him great anxiety. He felt jealous of the people who were included in the book. Now the usual therapeutic response would have been to search for the reasons Jesse was so insecure and jealousy-ridden. Was it his mother? An early love affair? My interest was in getting rid of his consuming jealousy. The whys, if he wished (and he didn't particularly), could come later when he had more time. Here, for an extreme example, is Jesse's jealousy hierarchy.

•

Jesse's Jealousy Hierarchy

0	He is on a vacation from his life. There are no scripts to consider, no shooting dates, he has nothing to do, except relax in a green meadow and watch the clouds in a blue sky.
20	His friend Lillian spends an unexplained hour with a writer.
30	His friend Mary didn't leave a message that she would be late for dinner.
45	A colleague at work turns down his offer of having dinner together.
60	Bill (whom he no longer loves) describes his personal relationships with new people.
70	He imagines that Jenny is going to spend the evening with someone else.
70	He meets Jenny and there is an unexpected distance between them. She doesn't really want to talk to him.
80	He imagines Charles playing erotic games with another man.
100	Charles does not love him, never loved him, is passionately in love with Matthew.

•

Of course Jesse, with his myriad, bisexual love affairs and obsessive jealousy, is not typical. But none of us is typical. However singular or within the bounds of convention, our love is still unique and wholly unusual in that it is ours. Jesse did thought-stopping, silent ridicule and positive image building. But it was graduated calming that gave him the objectivity to stand back from his multiple involvements and overcome the destructive force of his jealousy.

•

We all feel jealousy from time to time. It is when jealousy interferes with our lives that it becomes a subject for concern.

•

Marjory, twenty-two-year-old secretary. Marjory was in love with and jealous of her boss, Stanley. Stanley was ten years older than she. As in the usual boss-secretary relationship, he held power, authority and status over her. He would wait until the last possible minute at the end of the day before asking her, as if it had just occurred to him, "Well, what are you doing tonight?" Their relationship went on for three years. It became clear to her that it was not going to develop further when she learned that he was also having affairs with two other women. She saw him every day and she saw the two other women every day.

•

Marjory's Jealousy Hierarchy

0   She is a young girl riding a horse in the forest. The horse stops at a stream and drinks.

10 He gets a phone call from a woman she does not know. She picks up the phone.

20 He has a date with another woman.

40 She calls him very late at night and he is not at home.

60 She calls him and he says it is not a good time to talk.

70 She pictures him having a sexual relationship with another woman.

80 He falls in love with another woman. ·

•

Marjory had some difficulty in doing deep muscle relaxation. The pressure of her job and constantly seeing Stanley throughout the day made her very tense. However, once she learned to relax she was able to reduce her jealousy fairly quickly. Toward the end of the graduated calming process, she was able to picture Stanley making love with another woman and say, "Frankly, Stanley, I don't give a damn," and mean it. She was also able to go to her person- 65 nel department and ask them to switch her job, something she was reluctant to do while she was in love with and jealous of Stanley.

●

Please note that the scene listed at zero is the scene each person uses to help get down to zero jealousy. Not everybody uses a scene; some find deep muscle relaxation sufficient. Here are two more lists.

●

Kelly, thirty-three-year-old actress in daytime television serials. She was in love with a man who had been married. He was not in love with her, but strung her along. She found that she had to stop feeling jealous over him to stop being in love with him.

●

Kelly's Jealousy Hierarchy

0	Watching the merry-go-round in the park.
10	Seeing him with his children from his former marriage.
25	Hearing him talk about people he knew when he was married.
30	His giving his children presents.
35	His ex-wife still has his name.
50	On his income tax form, he checks the box marked "married" and lists his children as dependents.
60	Meeting people that he knew when he was married.
60	He sends money to his ex-wife.
60	His old possessions, like pots and pans and silverware, from his former marriage.
80	He gets a letter by mistake addressed to his wife.
95	People talking to her about what a wonderful marriage he had.

95   Him talking to his former wife.

100   Talking to his former wife herself.

•

And finally, a hierarchy from Ken, a sixty-year-old construction worker who had left his wife of many years for a thirty-four-year-old woman who soon left him. As you can imagine, when the younger woman left him, he felt a whole complex of emotions, among them jealousy over the younger woman.

•

Ken's Jealousy Hierarchy

20   She has a beer with someone else.

35   She goes away for the weekend.

45   She goes away for the weekend with a man on business.

60   She tells Ken that she thinks she is falling in love with someone else.

70   She goes out with someone else on his (Ken's) birthday.

80   Canceling their Christmas plans together.

As you see, you don't have to span the spectrum from zero to one hundred. As in your thought-stopping list, your jealousy hierarchy doesn't have to be anything except yours.

Graduated Calming

Graduated calming is simply going up your own anxiety hierarchy, slowly, carefully, while deeply relaxed, one step at a time and repeatedly imagining the lowest scene on your hierarchy until you can experience that scene, in your imagination, without anxiety. As soon as you can experience a scene, without anxiety, in your imagination, you can experi- 67 ence that scene in reality without anxiety. As long, of course, as the scene does not have real danger in it.

Having established your emotional history and your own anxiety hierarchy, a behavior therapist would begin graduated calming with deep muscle relaxation. Care would be taken to give you the pleasure and safety of being deeply relaxed. Nothing will harm you, nothing will disturb your tranquility.

Then gradually, sensitively, the therapist will, by degrees, expose you to those things, situations, people, emotions, or environments that now cause you anxiety until you can experience them without feeling anxiety.

Graduated calming is very much like the way a young mother (or father) might teach her child not to be afraid of the sea. The first day, while holding her child close to her, she shows her child the sea from the top of a dune. The next day they walk toward the sea while she holds and reassures her child. The next day they come closer. And so on, closer and closer (graduated approach), constantly reassuring her child (repetition in a low-anxiety environment) until the child becomes familiar with the strange new environment and feels relaxed enough to get his feet wet.

The theoretical basis for graduated calming rests on the fact that jealousy is learned. If you can re-experience something that causes jealousy *without* feeling jealous, there is a new learning that goes on. If you can face those events (even in your imagination) in a relaxed state, in a systematic way, your jealousy will be diminished.

Any stress during graduated calming is counterproductive. So you should be very conservative in drawing up your anxiety hierarchy. If you are not sure whether to assign a thirty or a fifty to a scene, by all means give it a fifty. Because, if you experience a high level of anxiety while you are deeply relaxed, it will destroy your relaxed state. And, equally important, graduated calming works one step at a time. Go up the scale gradually, cautiously, over a period of time. Take it one step at a time. The relaxation inhibits anxiety. But relaxation can only inhibit anxiety if anxiety is kept low. To conquer your large jealousies you first must conquer your small ones. Conquering small jealousies generally has the effect of diminishing the larger ones. Conquer a ten, and a ninety tends to move down to eighty.

Here is how you might go through graduated calming yourself. First, relax with deep muscle relaxation. In order to do graduated calming, you have to be at zero, completely relaxed, so that your deep muscle relaxation will be strong enough to compete with and to win out over those feelings of jealousy. You may also find low lights and soft music helpful. Be sure you are in a comfortable, quiet place where you will not be interrupted. When you are perfectly relaxed at zero, imagine as clearly and with as much detail as possible a place, a person or scene that is very low on your scale, say ten or twenty. Imagine that for five or ten seconds or until you begin to feel some anxiety. Then shut it off and relax for some twenty or thirty seconds or however long it takes to get back to zero. You might like to have a pleasant relaxing thought handy to replace the thought that causes jealousy (your zero thought or a particularly serene thought from the pleasurable images in your thought-stopping list). Other examples of a pleasant, relaxing thought might be a tall pine tree or a kite fluttering in the sky, or riding in a hot air balloon on a summer day, or the applause after you've starred in a play. These reassuring thoughts, like Linus's blanket, are comforting things to have.

Here are some other aids in getting back down to zero: Exhale slowly, saying the word "calm." Count your fingers without moving them or looking at them. Focus on the texture beneath your fingers without moving them. Count your toes without moving them or looking at them. Get a sense of where your knees are without looking at them or touching them. Picture your forehead as being perfectly smooth without any lines or wrinkles. Focus your attention 69 on your knuckles or your ankles without looking at them. When you get back down to zero again (and take as much time as you need to get there), relax, and stay there a few moments.

Next return to that same thought that is ten or twenty on your jealousy hierarchy. Should you feel the first hint of jealousy, erase the thought, and go back to deep relaxation with your relaxing thought. You will need to repeat that scene again.

The point is to repeat the process until the scene does not cause you any jealousy anymore. When you can imagine the scene without any negative feelings (without jealousy or anxiety), continue to imagine the scene for about twenty seconds. Hold the thought for another five or ten seconds (you might want to hold the scene for a longer time and savor how relaxed you feel with the scene). Then erase the scene.

Relaxation competes with jealousy; you can't feel both at once. Be sure you introduce jealousy very slowly and at a low level so that relaxation always wins. Again, when you weaken the lower levels of jealousy on your scale, you also diminish the higher levels.

When you are rid of feeling jealous over the ten or twenty scene on your scale, you can move up to the scene you labeled twenty or thirty. Always be careful to cut off the thought as soon as you feel the least bit jealous and do not repeat the thought again until you are back at zero in deep relaxation. And always be careful to move up only ten or, at the most, twenty points on the scale for the next scene. You want to be sure that relaxation always wins and jealousy always loses so that relaxation is learned and jealousy is unlearned. If there is a large gap in your jealousy hierarchy that requires you to make a big jump while doing graduated calming, make up a scene that causes the appropriate amount of jealousy. For example, if your jealousy hierarchy has a gap in it like this:

10   Hearing him talking to someone on the phone.

20

30

40   He says he's going to meet a woman. You know the woman is attracted to him.

Try to imagine a scene that would cause you to feel at twenty and a scene that would cause you to feel at thirty on your jealousy scale. Twenty could be that you find out he is talking to a woman on the phone. Thirty might be that you realize the woman on the phone is someone you know is attracted to him. The point is to keep the graduated calming process as gradual and as easy as possible. It's difficult to go from a ten to a forty and still have relaxation win over jealousy. And the fact that it is not a "real" scene won't interfere with the graduated calming process. Graduated calming is not an overnight cure. But daily practice can bring a real change in two weeks. I realize that doing graduated calming on your own is not easy. There is a good deal to learn and it takes repetition and time. On the other hand, it is the first cure for jealousy that works. And being rid of jealousy with all its debilitating depression and waste of energy and time is a great emotional lift that can change and improve your life enormously. And if you are afflicted with jealousy, you have to get rid of it to break the emotional bonds that tie you to the person you want to fall out of love with.

Exercises

Deep Muscle Relaxation

1. Practice deep muscle relaxation, as described in this chapter, two times a day.
2. Also, focus on relaxing a small area, such as your neck or your forearm, for five minutes every day.
3. Every time you pick up a telephone, sit down to eat, or come to a stoplight or stop sign or crosswalk, take a few brief seconds to focus on relaxing a finger, knee, biceps, or some other small part of your body to help integrate relaxation into your life.
4. Once you've done two weeks of deep muscle relaxation twice daily, you may well not have to tense your muscles before you relax them. Focusing on observing and relaxing will help you to relax in a shorter time.

Graduated Calming

1. Relax until you are at zero.
2. Bring on or imagine the first scene from your jealousy hierarchy.
3. If you feel *any* anxiety or jealousy, erase the scene.
4. Go back to relaxing until you get to zero.
5. Bring the scene on again and continue imagining it, but again, if you feel any anxiety or jealousy, erase the scene.
6. Go back to relaxing until you get to zero.
7. When you can continue imagining the scene for about twenty seconds and still feel yourself so relaxed that you stay at zero, savor and enjoy how relaxed you feel with this scene. Then erase it.
8. Continue relaxing.
9. Continue the whole process (at a later time if you wish) with the next scene on your hierarchy.

6

Repulsion

You may wish to skip this chapter. It's about an ugly technique I rarely use. The overwhelming chances are you don't need it, unless after practicing all the other previous techniques you still feel a strong physical attraction for your former love.

The technical name of the technique I call repulsion is covert sensitization, as developed by Dr. Cautela. It is sometimes used in behavior therapy for alcoholism, smoking and overeating. I've found that it is also useful in neutralizing physical attraction.

There's no explaining physical attraction: It happens. It goes way beyond the way people look. A certain scent, a light in the eyes, a kind of smile, memories and vague longings are the elusive stuff of attraction. Call it magic or chemistry, however you define physical attraction, it is as real and wonderful as anything we ever feel. It can also be extremely persistent. In that rare instance when, after doing thought-stopping, silent ridicule and graduated calming, a person still feels a strong physical attraction for someone who does not or cannot love him or her, or for someone in a destructive relationship, it may be necessary to use repulsion.

Repulsion is a radical means of breaking the power of physical attraction. It teaches you to associate physical

73

contact with that person with something so negative that it's repulsive. Oddly enough, repulsion doesn't make you feel that that person is repulsive, it simply weakens whatever that magnet is that so attracts you.

Here is how it works. Draw up a short list of the things that are most repulsive to you. You don't need more than one or two things, but the smellier, slimier and nastier, the better. What is the foulest thing you can think of to see, touch, smell and sit in? Some of the most common examples are: excrement, sewer flow, flies, vomit, blood, cockroaches, snakes, garbage, manure and pus. One of the most vivid I've heard is "ooze from a dead rat."

Find a quiet place where you won't be disturbed. Then think of a scene in which you are about to have physical contact with the person you loved. You are about to touch, embrace or kiss that person and just as you get close to him or her you see and smell that he or she is covered with ooze or excrement or whatever you find most repulsive. You pull back, not wanting to touch or kiss excrement, and as you turn away, suddenly everything is gone, including the person. The air is clear and sweet and you feel fresh and new.

Here are two examples of how repulsion worked for two people who, even after thought-stopping, silent ridicule and desensitization, felt a strong physical attraction for someone who did not love them.

•

Bart, twenty-seven years old, worker on a loading dock. Bart had gotten married right after high school. He was a powerful man and to support himself and his wife, he had taken the best paying job he could find, loading produce onto trucks at a huge depot for a supermarket chain. The loading dock was as long as a football field. Crates of produce, stacked on wooden pallets, would be continually brought out from the warehouse. His job was to carry the crates into the truck and stack them inside. The crates were all different sizes and shapes, and fitting them together so they didn't fall or crush one another was almost an art. He called it "filling empty trucks with full boxes." When he was promoted to "checker," the person who keeps inventory and makes sure each truck gets the right goods (thirty-seven crates of Maine potatoes, seventeen crates of escarole), it seemed much easier work. All he had to lift was a pencil and clipboard. And it was an extra ninety-five cents an hour. It was also boring. He measured his day by the clock. "Fifteen minutes to coffee break." "One hour to lunch." "An hour and eighteen minutes to coffee break." With three children to feed and monthly rent to pay, he felt trapped. One escape was fantasizing about playing pro football, driving fast cars, or women. He met Mary Ellen in the lunchroom. They both felt an almost electric attraction to each other. They would meet after work, or on weekends or late at night. As their affair went on and their lovemaking became more elaborate and inventive, the physical attraction they felt for each other grew even stronger. Inevitably people began to talk. The men he worked with made jokes about it, and when they met in the lunchroom there were loud guffaws. It was Mary Ellen who ended the affair. She felt obligated to and was in love with the man she was living with. She hated the gossip and couldn't help but overhear it. She felt cheap. Bart, too, felt it was probably a good thing that it ended. He was very fond of his wife and his children and he did not want to hurt them. But while checking the crates, he would dream of the wonderful things that Mary Ellen could do with her mouth. His mind filled with the memory, the scent and the touch of her. And he saw her every day. And now that he could no longer make love to her, he really could not get her out of his mind. We did thought-stopping and silent ridicule. Thought-stopping was effective, but silent ridicule was not. He would try to picture her in a ridiculous situation or outfit, but she would seem just as sexy and desirable. The thought of her wearing her dirty work jeans and jacket to a fancy dinner at a friend's house or showing up at work 75 in a frilly, pink ballet outfit gave him an erection. Almost any thought of her gave him an erection. So we did repulsion. He pictured her covered with vomit, chunks of it caught in her hair, gobs of vomit on her face, steaming, dripping puke soaking her clothes. Whenever he first began to think of her he would picture her clothes or her body running with stinking vomit. It was strong medicine, but it worked. There were days when Bart couldn't eat his lunch and for a while he ate alone on the back of a truck. In a little over two weeks, Bart saw Mary Ellen as a pretty, attractive woman, but the mind-filling urge and desire that he had felt was now a memory rather than a continual torture.

•

Carla, thirty-eight-year-old housewife. When Carla first saw Michael, she didn't think or feel anything special about him. He was her bank's manager, one of any number of people she saw in her suburban town several times a week. When he asked her, one morning, to have a cup of coffee, she thought he wanted to reprimand her for her erratic, sometimes overdrawn, bank balance. And perhaps he did. However, they began to meet regularly for morning coffee, and then, secretly, became lovers. Since her son had just left for college, Carla felt liberated from a large part of her household chores and, at the same time, at loose ends because there was so much less to do around the house. Her husband commuted into the city, left early and was often late coming home. An "affair" had always had a romantic sound to Carla; she found the idea of it exciting. What she found unexciting was Michael, himself, in every way except physically. That was fine, she felt, because she didn't really want to become too involved with him. His lack of anything interesting to talk about, his uncurious mind, was a solid weight to balance against the fact that he was wonderful in bed. What Carla hated was the deception, the lies she had to tell her friends, the lies she had to tell her husband, the frustration at not being able to tell anyone. She

76

found that she was cutting friends off when they had something important to tell her. She found she was beginning to
resent her husband's mild inquiries about her day. She also
felt guilty. It made her feel small and cheap. And while she
could appreciate and applaud the "sexual revolution," she
discovered that she really was happiest with her home and
her husband. Falling out of love with Michael was easy.
She doubted she ever was really in love with him, apart
from the kind of giddy, schoolgirl crush that she would
sometimes feel. Shaking his physical attraction was a
wholly different matter. She changed banks and made an
effort not to see him. Still he would crop up in her mind,
unwelcome but very real, when she was making love to her
husband, or having coffee or driving to the supermarket.
She said she felt as if she was a sort of Michael "junkie" —
that her body had developed a craving for him. Thought-
stopping kept him out of her mind, but still her body ached
for him. She pictured him in the bank wearing a bow tie
that lights up. She pictured him with his hair in curlers (he
was very dignified and precise about his appearance) and
she pictured him as a clerk in a pornography store. Those
scenes had some effect, but they weren't strong enough to
overcome her desire to feel his touch. I told Carla about repulsion and she agreed to try it. She pictured Michael, who
was so fastidious, with excrement coming out of his mouth
and ears, coming out of his penis, spreading great stinking
stains all over his shirt and trousers, gobbets of excrement
on his banker's suit. It was, as she said, enough. She still
sees Michael from time to time in town, where they ex-
change pleasantries and go their separate ways.

The human imagination has great power. For repulsion
to work, you have to use that power. You have to see, smell
and almost feel the nasty, foul sight, odor and texture of the
excrement. As in thought-stopping, repulsion is an emotional learning and unlearning. In learning to turn away   77

from that person physically, you unlearn the physical attraction you feel for that person. To break those emotional links you have to practice repulsion some fifteen times in a session once a day and every single time you begin to feel a physical longing for that person. It's not a pretty technique, it's ugly. And it almost seems an unfair thing to do to someone you love. But physical attraction that can't be satisfied, or causes emotional harm when it is, is unfair too. In an all-out effort to stop loving someone, you may need an all-out weapon.

Exercises

1. Fifteen times a day, bring on a scene wherein you are about to touch, embrace or kiss the person you loved.
2. When you get very close to that person, notice and smell that he or she is covered with an obnoxious substance such as vomit, excrement or blood.
3. Turn away from that person and imagine how clear and fresh the air is, and picture a fresh spring scene — or any other pleasurable scene you choose (a new lover, a mountain, the sea, Robert Redford) — to reward yourself for turning away.
4. Any time you see the person or begin to feel a physical longing for that person, repeat steps one through three.

PART TWO

... And in Again

7

Intimacy

You're vulnerable now. You've endured a great deal of pain. Chances are your ego has suffered. And you face the difficult task of rebuilding your life without your former love. What I want to suggest are some ways of beginning again that should make your life easier. Perhaps not now, but soon you will feel the need to share again, to be with somebody who understands and appreciates what you do. There is a paradox here. It may be very difficult to trust someone new if you've been deeply hurt. At the same time, you may want very much to trust someone, to be close and have that wonderful sense of intimacy, of being loved as well as loving.

Being Intimate with Someone New

It is difficult and you can take all the time you need. After being close to a person for some time, there are all those things that are missing with a new person, all those old private signals, words, jokes and memories that don't really mean anything to a new person. Those new people and places you may have to meet and deal with on your own terms. It may be you were a part of a scene that is closed to you now. A circle of mutual friends you used to have may no longer be available to you. So there's a good chance that there's more involved than simply finding the right person. In other words, now that you are on your own, you will need to make your own way in the world. And that can be an intimidating thought.

Loving someone new can be the best way to get over a broken or dead-end relationship. I don't mean to recommend that you seek a new love as a cure-all or that you try to re-create an old relationship with someone else. Loving someone new is a new experience. It is a chance to begin again and learn from the mistakes you may have made in the past. But a new love is unlikely to be easy for you now.

One way to ease the awkwardness is to ask someone to give you a little help. Ask someone you know and trust (a friend, a brother, a sister, a fellow student or someone at work), someone who you feel has capabilities where you feel less than strong. Ask him or her to help with specific details such as, "How do I find a class or course on a subject I'm interested in?" Or, "I'm shy about going to a new class. Would you come with me the first time?" Or, "How do I say no when a man asks me out and I don't want to go, but I don't want to offend him either?" You might also ask your friend to rehearse things with you. It's most helpful to rehearse a phone call or a conversation, to try it out and get comfortable with it. Ask your guide to do it first. He or she becomes the model and then you do your own variations.

Suppose you have trouble starting a conversation. Ask your advisor for some ideas. In the meantime here are some examples a model might give you for conversation starters.

Model: "I've heard that's a really good book you're reading. I wonder if I might borrow it when you're finished. I'm one of those rare people who returns books."

Model: "I've never been here before. Do you know anything about the place?"

Model: "That's a cute dog. Did you knit him yourself?"

Model: "I can't really stop and talk right now. But I would like to see you sometime soon."

Model: "Excuse me for eavesdropping, but what you are saying sounds really interesting."

Model: "I'm sorry. I really don't want to see anybody this evening. Can I take a rain check?"

What you need to do is decide where you need help. And then ask your guide (or model or enabler or social tutor or buddy) for help. For example, "I can't have folks over for supper because I don't know what to serve them." Or, "How do I call someone and ask for a date? Where would I take her?" Your guide can give you the advice you need. It's remarkable how willing and glad most people are to give you their advice.

As for where you meet people, a few suggestions may be useful. Look for things and places that interest you. Is there a course (in adult education, at a college or high school) you'd like to take? Do you want to learn carpentry or weaving or tennis or how to dance the hustle? Do you want to become involved in politics, car racing, teaching children to read? Follow your own interests and you're bound to raise your chances of meeting someone who's interested in you. Of course, there are always singles bars and events. A while back, a man in New York, frustrated in his search for a bride, ran an ad in the *New York Times.* SINGLES BARS ARE GREAT, said the headline, IF YOU WANT TO STAY SINGLE. I don't mean to imply that you are or should be looking for a marriage partner. It's just that the not-so-happy hunting ground of singles bars is full of people from out of town on one-night business trips, others desperately looking for real love, noise, smoke and complete strangers. And, unless you're really looking for one-night stands and temporary affection, you really do take your chances. I'd 83 guess that you are better off taking things more slowly and doing things you feel good about.

But, whatever the scene or the place, you will probably feel somewhat socially awkward on your own. You seem to be missing part of yourself now that your former love is not there. It will take a while to feel whole on your own. Here's a technique that Dr. Wolpe calls in vivo (in real life) desensitization that we use for social awkwardness. It is based on the graduated calming technique you read about in the jealousy chapter.

As you recall, graduated calming was being relaxed, imagining a scene that caused you some small level of jealousy and/or anxiety and then erasing the scene from your mind and returning to a relaxed state. In vivo graduated calming is similar in principle, but different in practice. Suppose, for example, you feel uncomfortable about going to a party. You feel say thirty or forty on your anxiety scale. There could be a hundred reasons. You know a lot of people who will be there and you don't want to talk about your old love affair. You don't know anybody there. You feel you stick out like a sore thumb without your old partner. You haven't been out for days and you feel unattractive. You don't have the right clothes. The idea of a party depresses you. For any number of reasons, you don't want to go. Well, you can say no. You don't have to go. On the other hand, you might try going with a friend for just a short while. Go, stay three to five minutes, and leave if you feel uncomfortable. You don't have to talk to people. Simply go, experience the scene and leave. In vivo graduated calming means doing things slowly, gradually, to reduce your anxiety. The theory goes like this: When you can experience an anxiety-provoking scene in the presence of a comforting agent (a friend who goes with you, a reward to look forward to, just knowing you will leave soon), you diminish your anxiety. You can see the similarity to graduated calming. The difference is that you don't imagine and erase scenes, you physically enter and leave them. In both cases you emotionally unlearn your anxiety. The technique is infinitely variable. With three to four people you may stay twenty minutes. The next time you may stay an hour. You want to gradually build up until you are relaxed enough to walk into a strange group or place and feel relatively comfortable about it.

Thus far, I've been giving you rather generalized advice about how you might meet someone you could relate to. So much depends on your own situation. A sophomore in college jilted by her high-school sweetheart faces a vastly different set of circumstances from a businessman who's been widowed after thirty years of marriage. But should you find someone you'd like to be close to, I can be much more specific.

Intimacy — being close, open, sharing, vulnerable and trusting — is the most rewarding kind of relationship. It is also, potentially, the most painful, because if you trust, you can be hurt. What I want to suggest is a specific program for gaining and sustaining intimacy. Because intimacy is learned, you have to learn to be close, open, sharing, and so on, all over again with a new person. First a general statement, then six specifics.

Begin in a graduated, tentative, testing manner. Go slowly. Take small, graduated steps in sharing yourself with another person. And evaluate how responsibly the new person can handle what you are giving. It takes time for someone to know you. Don't tell all your secrets and desires and fantasies at once. You want to be able to see how well you are being accepted. You don't want to be hurt because the person does not live up to your hopes, or because you don't fulfill someone else's image of who you ought to be. Probably no endeavor on earth begins with higher hopes in the face of fewer chances for success than new love affairs. So keep a clear eye open to see if he or she ridicules or criticizes you for giving and sharing. If that's 85 the case, you should seriously consider ending the relationship. If, on the other hand, it feels good and right and has a chance of growing, here are six things that will help your relationship grow stronger and more loving.

What You Can Do for Love

Say "I"

"I want." "I need." "I feel." "I want to give you." Take responsibility for what you think and what you feel. It will make things so much clearer. The temptation is to say, "You make me feel," "You hurt me." Your feelings are your own. And by saying "I" instead of "you," you take responsibility for your feelings. You avoid shifting the responsibility. You avoid attacking and putting down. It makes you both stronger. For example:

> Instead of: "You hurt me."
> Say: "I feel hurt."
>
> Instead of: "You never give me enough affection."
> Say: "I need more affection."

Saying "I" cuts out so much useless debate. What you feel is valid. What someone did or said to cause that feeling is debatable.

Don't Guess, Ask

It's so easy to assume you know what another person thinks. And so often wrong. It's hard enough to be truly aware of what you think and feel at any given moment. Other people are equally complex. And changing. When you say, "I know you really want to," you really don't know. When you say, "You don't want to see me," you may

86

or may not be right. But you certainly don't know all the reasons why. Guessing clutters communication between two people. "You're saying that because you . . ." is an invitation to more pointless conjecture. And all those roundabouts of guessing and second-guessing are easily avoided. Instead of projecting what you think the other person feels, *ask!*

And leave your questions open-ended and unloaded. For example, instead of saying, "You're angry with me because" (guessing), or "Are you angry with me for doing that?" (loaded question), simply ask, "What do you feel about that?"

A person sits across from you and frowns, and you might respond, "You seem angry today." Angry? Consider just a few of the possibilities. Instead of being angry, the other person might: (1) have a headache; (2) have had a restless night; (3) have had a troublesome day at work; (4) be remembering that he forgot to pick up the laundry; (5) have an itch at the corner of her mouth; (6) have overeaten; (7) be worried about the rent; and on ad infinitum. There are so many complex possibilities behind the simplest of human gestures. If you want to know, don't guess. Ask and be sure.

No Put-downs, Dumping or Criticism

There's a form of friendly American affection that expresses itself as a put-down. "Hey. I didn't know somebody your age could do that." It passes for humor. But the undercurrent is destructive. You think you're saying, "I don't mind that you're old," and what the other person may be hearing is, "You're old. You won't be able to do that much longer." Try to avoid saying things like "You never . . ." "Why don't you ever . . ." "You're always late . . ." Be kind in your expression. It doesn't hurt. I don't mean you should mask your feelings with sweetness. 87

Just say what you feel without making it a direct criticism. In the end it may mean that you simply have to get used to not saying some of the things you are used to saying.

Give Compliments

Compliments, genuine compliments, feel as good as the rays of the sun. When you see or feel something you like in a person, say so. Make it a focus. "Oh, I like the way you do that." I don't mean that you should give false praise. But if you like someone, and you think about it, there will be lots to praise.

Praise doesn't have to be lavish. It's usually easier to receive it if it's not. It does have to be genuine. And it is best when it is specific. Not, for example, "You're handsome." But, "I love your blue eyes." Praise can be very small and still very valuable. For example, "I'm glad we had a few minutes together" can be very good to hear.

No "You Should"s or "You Shouldn't"s

"You should not be late all the time." "You should dress better." "You shouldn't talk so much." "You should be less enthusiastic." "You shouldn't drink so much." "You shouldn't have those kind of friends."

If you find yourself feeling a number of shoulds and shouldn'ts about someone, you might think about whether it is a suitable relationship to be in. It just might be that what you are really saying is that you want to be in a relationship with someone else. Love is accepting someone for what they are, not what they should be. The truth is that adults don't change much. And they certainly don't change as a result of reminders of what they should or should not do. If you really do want to change someone (and as I say, it's both risky and rare), the best chance you have is in focusing on their strengths and enhancing their self-image.

88

That's one way people change in therapy. An important footnote is that many people do change through intimacy and loving relationships. Not through scolding.

Empathy

Empathy means identifying and listening when there's a problem instead of offering solutions and advice. When, at the end of the day, for example, you're told, "I'm tired," you could easily offer the following counsel: "Well, you shouldn't work so hard," or "You shouldn't let them take advantage of you," or "You should plan better," or "Get more sleep," or "You're not eating well enough," or "You need more exercise." All of which is bound to make a person more tired. Empathy would be realizing yourself what it feels like to be tired after a difficult day, and saying things like, "I'm sorry you're tired. What happened?" or "Let me get you a beer," or "How about a backrub?" or "Would you like a hot bath?" or "What could I do to help you feel better?"

Let's take another example. Your partner says, "I'm upset." There are an infinite number of ways to respond to that. It's easy to try and smooth over the situation, as if with a little advice the situation will go away. You could say, "Don't be upset. It's trivial," or "Forget it," or "You're too sensitive," or "Don't let people get to you like that." Particularly infuriating is the objective, rational approach: "Just look at it rationally and you'll see why it's silly to be upset." On the other hand, instead of contributing to the aggravation, you could help to relieve it. "What's upsetting?" "Why?" "How come?" "How can I help?" "Tell me more." "Let me rub your neck."

Swinging Slowly in the New Scene

Ever since the pill and the technological evolution in contraception, the whole world seems to have changed about
sex. It's freer, more casual and everybody seems to be
doing it. Everywhere the "new scene" exerts its pull. Its
promise of pleasure without guilt, fun with no regrets,
sounds suspiciously easy but worth a try. Especially when
you're emotionally bruised and lonely.

I see a lot of battered refugees from the new scene. And
while I don't condemn or recommend the new scene, I think
you ought to know that it hardly exists. Of course there are
lots of singles bars and clubs and weekends. And they
sometimes lead to something far more interesting than
home-alone-again. And there are healthy, joyful people
who have sex as recreation. But for the great majority, for
almost everyone, there is a great clanging dissonance between what we *think* is the new scene and our own deeply
held attitudes about the way two people treat each other,
about what love is and what it's supposed to be. It's almost
as if you, as a stranger, opened up a door on a roomful of
happy, joking, talking people — swingers, it would appear,
in the new scene. And you called out, "Hey, who's at home
here?" And suddenly the room was empty. It's almost as if,
for all the crowds clamoring to be part of sexual freedom,
once you get there, nobody's there. Because that conflict
between what you *think* is supposed to happen and what in
your heart of hearts you *feel* should happen creates an awful
mess in communication. To take just one typical example.
Recently a successful, confident man came to me with
problems of impotence in going to bed with women on the
first date. "Well, why do you do it, then?" I asked. He said,
"That's what women expect these days." Women say the
same thing. "I have to because it's expected." So look at
the mess they're both in. He has too much anxiety to make

love right away. And she doesn't want to. But they both go ahead because they think that's what it's all about now. Nobody talks about it. He's worried about performance. She resents it and they *still* don't talk about it. They both make these grand assumptions about what the other person feels. Swingers rarely feel all that swinging. Most of us have a reservoir of suspicion about instant sex because we were told when we were young kids that you only have sex when you are married and then only with one person.

Even students in college have trouble with the rush into bed. They were also brought up by parents who told them that promiscuity is sleazy. They may feel less guilt than kids of earlier generations. But there is still an undercurrent of anxiety about the conflict between what they do and what they feel deep down they ought to do.

As a general rule, most of us feel that everybody else can swing. It's only ourselves who have trouble managing the ropes. The fact is, most people are like ourselves.

As you can tell by now, I think that most people cheat themselves out of a whole range of necessary, precious, gorgeous experiences if they rush into sex. For some people, it is fine. But I've found that most people go directly from A to Z without any stops along the way, creating anxiety and tension for themselves.

Just consider, for a moment, all the possible anxieties that people might carry into a new experience.

1. *Performance Anxieties:* Will I be able to have an erection? Will I last long enough? Will I have an orgasm or will I have to fake it? Will I lubricate or be too dry? Will I measure up to his/her other lovers? Am I any good as a lover? What do I do?

2. *Specific Anxieties:* Will I look okay nude? Will I get stuff on my hands? Do I have to touch his . . . her . . . ? Oral sex? Being looked at? Looking foolish? Losing control? Pain of penetration? Odor?

3. *General Anxieties:* Sex is dirty. What would my mother and/or father think? I'm betraying my old partner. This isn't love.

It may be possible that there are people who feel all these anxieties. Just as there may be some people who feel none of them. Most people feel one or more of them. And going straight to bed with a new acquaintance is bound to aggravate anxieties. This, in turn, reduces or even prohibits the joy.

First Experience

For all the "new scene" traumas, and all the anxieties, and all your emotional wounds, there will be a "first time" with someone you care about. Here is a program I developed with Dr. William K. Kirby, director of the Wesley-Westminster Foundation at Princeton University.

First, a law: Your first experience with a new person is like your very first experience.

You have to learn again. If you bring an old lovemaking agenda to a new lovemaking experience, it is going to get in the way. All your old moves and secret phrases, all the touches and places that used to turn someone else on, are for someone else.

Take your time.

Please, take your time. Don't let one of the best times of lovemaking be taken from you. There are years ahead for sexual lovemaking. You need time to build up intimacy and trust and reduce each other's anxiety. Lots of people rush into making love because they're attracted to someone and they want to do what's expected of them. Or they feel it's something to be gotten over with at the beginning. I suggest a long period where there is a build-up, where you get to know each other. It can be the sweetest time of all. Remember "making out" when you were a kid, that delicious temptation and desire. It's still true.

So often now, I see sex being used as a replacement for intimacy. People think that if they've made love, they're close. They leave out so much. And they find great gaping holes in their relationship later — empty places in terms of knowing who the other person is, what they feel, want, where they're going, what they like in terms of specific sexual things. They leave out the whole range of kissing and petting and the high arousal of exploring slowly and touching a real person instead of a stranger. They leave out the delicious time of teaching and learning . . . a process so complex and open-ended it could take a whole lifetime. They leave out seduction, that feeling of being intensely desired, that excitement of chasing after what you intensely desire. They leave out romance. So many people say that's what's missing in their lives. Even people who are into and enjoy experimental sex say, oh, they miss romance in their lives. And romance can be more than the most important ingredient for enjoying sex, it's really one of the best foundations for trusting and loving and enduring the erosion of time.

Ah, and they miss the laughter. I was once asked in a TV interview if I could give just one and only one piece of advice about sex, what would it be? And I said, "Laughter, laughter in the bedroom." It's hard to laugh with a stranger in the nude. But sex is always full of awkward moments. And you need time together before you can see those awkward positions, late or early ejaculations, false starts or calamitous distractions as hilarious or funny or endearing occasions instead of as disasters. Our expectations and hopes are so large in front of strangers. It's so much easier to feel at ease with someone you know and know you can trust.

And then, again, there is anxiety — yours and the other person's. Erotic feelings can overcome anxiety, but only slowly, one step at a time. I don't mean to say there isn't or can't be good sex early. Clearly there can be and is. It's just 93 that the odds are overwhelmingly improved if you take your time.

But if you don't rush into the expected, if, for the first time, you have a weekend, a honeymoon, or a room all to yourselves, what is the alternative?

A Sensual Holiday

A sensual holiday (a concept I developed with Dr. Kirby) can be an hour, a day, a week, or even a year when you decide to leave your old routines and roles behind and begin to know each other sensually, to teach and to learn how to be intimate. Let's say it is your first time together, and you both want to become lovers.

I'd suggest that you begin with a ban on intercourse — that the two of you agree that for the night or a week or even a year you will not have intercourse together. I know it sounds drastic and that it will be difficult to abstain. But it's good for building up the excitement, tantalization and pleasure. And when you both decide later that you can't wait any longer, that intercourse is irresistible, and you break the ban, that's fine. Breaking the ban almost adds to the enjoyment. And it's very different from thinking, "Tonight's the night. And I'm going to do it, no matter what. And I should do it, I've got to do it, and it has to be great." Putting a ban on something sexual can lower your anxiety and increase your pleasure. You might say it's like putting the lid on the cookie jar. It makes you hungry for what you cannot have. A ban on touching genitals, for example, leads you to seek pleasure in caressing other parts of your bodies. And a ban on taking off clothes can be incredibly tantalizing. If you have a performance anxiety, a ban can help reduce it. A man who is worried about having an erection can put a ban on having an erection. And since he's not supposed to (he doesn't "have to") have an erection he can

94

relax and enjoy himself. A woman worried about having an orgasm might feel more at ease with a ban on orgasms.

Part of a sensual holiday is teaching each other to focus on sensuality and learning to de-emphasize performance. Here are three sensual awareness training activities that you can take turns doing. The first one is touching and kissing the other person solely for your own pleasure. This is a chance to touch and feel and kiss wherever you like . . . to try a little massaging, to trace a vein, and so on. Your partner has an obligation to tell you when you make him or her nervous or uncomfortable. Once you know that — that your partner will stop you if he or she doesn't like something that you are doing — you can feel entirely free to explore and enjoy.

Next, try giving as much pleasure as humanly possible. The other person has to help you do this by teaching you how and where, how firm or gentle, how long or soft a stroke, when and how and where he or she likes to be kissed. That puts all the responsibility on the teacher (the person who's getting the pleasure) for getting the utmost pleasure. Because you have to be shown what your partner wants. When it's your turn to teach, make believe you are Queen Cleopatra or the King of England and you want and deserve as much pleasure as possible. You can teach verbally, and nonverbally. You can put your hands on the other person's hands to guide them, indicating where, how and how firmly. Or simply tell your partner what you wish or guide your partner's head to where you'd like to be kissed.

The third activity is simply focusing on what you feel, to become acutely aware of the temperature and texture under your fingers. You might focus on whether the place you are touching is smooth or warm or moist or tense or relaxed. You might also focus on signs of pleasure, such as breathing or movement in your partner.

One very important point a lot of people miss is creating a romantic mood. Music, dinner by candlelight, talking, walking in the moonlight, swimming in the nude, and talking some more, all help to make the experience more delicious.

Bathing together is a wonderful idea. Soap is a great conductor of sensation. Fool around with the slippery soap and you find all kinds of nooks and crannies. You can focus on soaping each other all over and over the genitals . . . feel what it feels like to . . . and to be . . . discover what he or she likes and where and how.

Seduction is an art and a craft when it's played like a game between two people. One person sets out to seduce the other person. This is especially good for women because women are likely to have been brought up to be the passive resister in seduction. It can be a fine turn-on for a woman to be assertive, with words and gestures, teasings and come-ons (not teasing to hurt, teasing to enhance arousal), music, dancing for someone, stripping someone, stripping for someone, maybe even a little bondage where the other person is not allowed to take part and just sits back and lets it happen, until you tell your partner to participate. Needless to add, seduction can be a fine turn-on for a man.

The last activity is simply to ask for something new. It might be you ask to have your back rubbed or your hair stroked. It might be, "I've always wanted to make love on the beach. Would you like to try that?" Or, "I wonder if it'd be good to try making love standing up." Notice that the request is tentative, not demanding. It's an exercise in being assertive and in sharing. "I wonder how you'd feel about keeping the lights on. I've always wanted to."

We've come a long way in these last few pages from the first tentative, cautious steps of a first experience. And yet it would be marvelous if you could keep some of the magic of that first experience in your relationship. That's why a sensual holiday is a good idea not only to create intimacy in the first place, but possibly also to do wonders for a long-established relationship.

8

Orgasmic Reconditioning

Sometime in the near future: It's your favorite time of day, you are comfortable, relaxed, and with someone who is very fond of you. And yet you find yourself, almost against your will, holding back, not just physically, but emotionally. There are reasons, certainly. You're still conscious of the pain of the last relationship. You're shy. And how can you be sure you're really fond of this new person.

Of course, you should not rush into another relationship. You not only can afford to take your time, you need to take your time and savor your life alone for a while. Yet it sometimes happens that you meet someone, and it's right, but you're not. Or, rather, something seems to stand between you and the new person.

Orgasmic reconditioning is a technique for transferring physical attraction from a former lover to a new one, particularly when the fantasy of your former partner keeps interfering with your caring more deeply for the new person. And particularly when recurring sexual fantasies of your former lover make it difficult to stop loving him or her. The technique is specifically designed for treating sexual problems with a new person caused by feelings of betrayal and guilt (I'm betraying my old relationship by beginning a new one). Any negative emotion (guilt, anxiety, anger, depression) inhibits sexual pleasure and can prevent arousal, erection, excitement, lubrication and orgasm. And so, too, can the memories of another person.

Orgasmic reconditioning is a new method (based on a technique developed by Dr. John Marquis) that I've been using successfully in "falling out of love" therapy over the past four years. I've demonstrated in previous chapters several different kinds of emotional learning and unlearning. But emotionally transferring your physical affection from a previous lover to a new one through the exercise of a specific technique is very new. And the fact that masturbation is at the heart of orgasmic reconditioning is bound to create controversy and skepticism. Many people still feel that the word masturbation is an ugly, even dirty, word. So, before I discuss the technique, I'd like to trace the origin and the history of masturbation's unclean reputation. It goes far beyond the word itself to our deepest feelings about sex and about ourselves.

Say self-love, self-exploration, individual personal excitation, or onanism and most people still become uneasy as soon as they realize what you're talking about. Why? It has been clinically proven, beyond any shadow of a doubt, that masturbation is not in and of itself harmful in any way. On the contrary, as we shall see, masturbation can be, in many ways, good for you. Where, then, does this deeply felt taboo and inhibition come from? Little babies find their toes and knees and everybody approves. But when the baby continues to explore and finds his or her genitals, the baby's hand is taken, or even slapped, away. The child is quickly diapered and forced to abstain. In this way, many of us learn that touching our own genitals is a shameful thing to do. And we learn that shame even before we have words to know what we are learning. Very early learning is very powerful. So powerful, in fact, that that early training may explain why, according to Kinsey's study *Sexual Behavior in the Human Female,* nearly 40 percent of the thousands of women interviewed have not masturbated. Many women never remember masturbating or never thought of masturbating or were scared that they might fail at masturbating. The theory is that they were taught that masturbation is taboo even before they learned to walk or talk.

Attitudes toward masturbation may be changing. But it remains one of our strongest taboos. The attitude that takes the hand away passes the antimasturbation ethic from one generation to the next. Besides our preverbal training, there is the shame and fear of being "caught." We're told by parents, teachers and friends that it's a dirty, nasty thing to do. Except for snickers and jokes, it's taboo to even talk about masturbation. Even people who can easily talk about other areas of sex at the dinner table would never talk about masturbation, particularly their own. Added to all this secrecy and shame, we have no models. When we're young, we watch people drive, bake cakes, play football, and so on. But do we ever see adults masturbate? It is true that children sometimes pass the word among themselves, "Hey, this is fun." But, by and large in our culture, the subject and the act of masturbation are surrounded by shame, guilt, fear, ignorance and taboo. In our culture, our adolescent heroes "score." Agent 007 seduces, he doesn't go home to masturbate. Masturbation is for losers; winners get the girl or guy. And yet, in our culture, masturbation is a normative (normal and natural) behavior. In 1948 and 1953, Kinsey showed that 93 percent of males and 62 percent of females have masturbated to orgasm at least once in their lives.

But, if masturbation is normal, if most people do masturbate, why do parents take their child's hand away when the child first feels its own genitals? The antimasturbation taboo does not, as many people believe, come from the Bible. The sin of Onan in the Old Testament was not masturbation, but coitus interruptus (interrupted intercourse). Under leviratic law, if you were a male, and your brother died, it was your lawful duty to marry and impregnate your widowed sister-in-law. So Onan was not masturbating, but rather performing his lawful duty until he withdrew from the fray and spilled his seed. The point of the law was to increase the numbers of the tribe, and Onan's sin was to diminish the tribe's chances for increase. In our own time of overpopulation, threatened famine and contraceptives, it does not seem an overly relevant tale. Although masturbation is not spoken against in the Bible, the Talmud does mention death as a punishment. But here again, it appears that the act itself is not the sin, but rather the sin is one of not propagating the tribe.

I expect there is a rich and rewarding field for a Ph.D. thesis on the origins of guilt in masturbation. What, for example, was Tissot's difficulty? Tissot, an eighteenth-century Swiss physician, is the first authoritative public figure that I can find who condemned masturbation. He was widely reported throughout Europe when he proclaimed that masturbation caused acne, consumption, epilepsy, gonorrhea, and insanity. In the next century, in England, William Acton, a physician, claimed that masturbation caused social isolation, impotence and insanity. At the time there were a number of methods to "help" people stop masturbating. Shocks to the penis were one treatment. If that proved unsuccessful, severing the nerves leading to the penis always worked. There were also handcuffs for children to wear to bed at night. And onanism rings with inward pointing stickers so that an erection was painful. And a metal glove (which had limited success). And a night bell rigged up to ring out the news of an erection. Two notes here. First, Tissot and Acton are not so much originators of repression as they are measures of the barbarity of their time regarding masturbation. I suppose nowadays we would call them thought leaders. But they were not alone. Cauterization of the genitals, clitoridectomy, castration and shock were common treatments for masturbation in the eighteenth and nineteenth centuries. Another note is that just as the first students of anthropology studied animals in the zoo, the first students of human behavior studied people held captive in "insane" asylums. And it was an understandable, although unhappy, conclusion to draw — seeing that the majority of "mad" people masturbate — that masturbation caused insanity. As we have seen, it was not until Kinsey's 1948 study that it was recognized that, simply, most people masturbate.

Richard von Krafft-Ebing, in the late nineteenth century, wrote a monumental catalogue of sexual deviation and crime called *Psychopathia Sexualis*. It was this otherwise invaluable, pioneering study of aberrant human behavior that gave credence to the notion that masturbation was not just an illness, but was also the major cause of sexual crimes. Masturbation, he said, was the primary cause of the sex-criminal aberrations documented in his book. He also claimed that the sins of masturbation are inherited. If your father masturbated, in other words, the chances are that you will be a sex criminal. Reading on in the history of sexual attitudes, you begin to appreciate what Victorian guilt really meant when you find that a highly respected and often quoted Victorian physician and educator, Elizabeth Blackwell, recommended that proper sex education for children should intensify and enlarge their feelings of shame about sex. Freud represented a small change in attitude. His opinion was that masturbation was immature and neurotic. That is, it was not an insane act, as was commonly supposed, but merely a perversion. It was tolerable in children as long as it did not happen very often and as long as they stopped when they reached puberty. In other words, masturbation was just sick, not criminal.

But opinion was and is slow to turn. It was over fifty years before Kinsey made his revolutionary disclosure that masturbation is normal behavior. Kinsey also documented the fact that masturbation is normal in animals and that animals duplicate human behavior in that more male animals masturbate than do females. And yet, despite Kinsey and many other researchers gathering information and publishing evidence that masturbation is a healthy, normal thing to do, the prevailing public opinion still seems to be that masturbation, while it doesn't cause blindness or hair on the palms, is shameful. And that masturbators are losers. The first person that I am aware of who recommended masturbation was Dr. Helena Wright. Dr. Wright said, in a book published in 1930, that masturbation is actually a very good way to learn about your own body. And she went on to describe several ways to masturbate as a healthy, important and worthwhile activity.

Masturbation *is* good and positive in many ways. After centuries of fear and suspicion, we are finally beginning to learn that masturbation not only does not cause blindness or hair on the palms, but does actually have a number of things to say in its favor. Let me list a few:

1. It's pleasurable. It feels good.
2. It's not illegal, fattening, or life-shortening. And it's free. (And you can't say that about too many of life's other pleasures.)
3. Masturbation teaches you about your own body and your own sexual responses. You tend to do what gives you the most pleasure. Knowing that, you can later teach someone else how to give you pleasure. Teaching your partner not only gives you access to more pleasure, it avoids leaving your partner in a vacuum, feeling ignorant and inadequate about what turns you on and what you are going to do next. This teaching, based on your own self-exploration, helps you both be more involved and assertive and loving. Moreover, orgasm is a very complex response. We are all very individual in our ways and means. There's no right way or wrong way. You have to learn your own way. Therefore, knowing yourself and your own needs and pleasures 103

helps you (and your partner) reach higher levels of excitement, pleasure, and joy.

Kinsey found the 87 percent of the women who had masturbated before marriage reached orgasm in intercourse in their first year of marriage. In sharp contrast, only 37 percent of the women who had *not* masturbated before marriage reached orgasm in intercourse in their first year of marriage. As Dr. Kinsey said, "There are very few instances, among our several thousand histories, of females who were able to masturbate to orgasm without becoming capable of similar responses in coitus." This directly refutes Freud's surmise that masturbation interferes with "mature" sexual functioning.

4. I have never known a couple who had the same sexual drive or needs. So often one wants to and the other doesn't. At those times, masturbation can be a caring and considerate compromise. It is also useful and practical when partners are separated or one partner is pregnant or simply tired.

5. To keep your sexual capabilities into your nineties, you need to stay sexually active. Masturbation doesn't use up sexual energy any more than running uses up the leg muscles. There will be times in your life when you will need masturbation to stay sexually active.

6. Self-reliance. Masturbation means that you can enjoy yourself, yourself. You don't have to rely on someone else for sexual pleasure. In fact, the strongest orgasm, physiologically speaking, is apt to be the one you have with yourself. Masters and Johnson, in studying over 1200 people, found this to be true for both men and women. The reason orgasm in masturbation is so often so intense is probably due to the instant feedback. You don't have to ask somebody to do this or that faster, slower, softer or harder.

7. If you are comfortable with your own "self-loving," you

are more likely to be comfortable with your children's natural exploratory needs and pleasures.

8. Masturbation is nonexploitive. You can enjoy sexual pleasures without making demands on someone else.

9. Masturbation is a good release of sexual tension. It's relaxing, it allows you to give a freer range to your sexual fantasies and, as a character in *The Boys in the Band* points out, you don't have to look your best.

10. And finally, masturbation can be a useful therapeutic technique. It's the most efficient way for women to learn to have an orgasm and for men to learn to delay ejaculation. And, as I mentioned at the beginning of this chapter and will come to again shortly, it's helpful in orgasmic reconditioning, changing the object of your desire.

The above paragraphs constitute an impressive list, I think, in favor of masturbation. But the list doesn't really end there. Although masturbation has had the reputation of causing any number of disorders, the reality is that *not* masturbating and our negative attitudes about masturbation are what cause harm. Let me begin with a theory. I suspect that a substantial part of our shame and guilt about sex can be traced to our feelings about masturbation. For most of us, masturbation is our first sexual experience. And, usually, at an early time in our lives, it is our only sexual experience. If we are made to feel shame and guilt at this first, very early level, if our hands are taken away and we are told it is bad and we should be ashamed, then it seems very likely that we would be conditioned to feel that sex is bad and something to be ashamed of. The shame is likely to be reinforced later when a youngster masturbates, but does not dare talk about it and cannot share his or her feelings about it.

Without strict clinical evidence, I would have to concede 105 that sexual guilt originating in masturbation is theory. But it is a highly probable theory. It is also true that fear of being found out may lead to rapid, hurried masturbation in males. Clinical evidence shows that this, in turn, leads to rapid or premature ejaculation.

Often women who do not or have not masturbated don't have orgasms.

If a woman has not explored her body and learned what pleases her and what does not, she may expect her partner to assume the burden of orchestrating the whole of lovemaking by himself. But no man automatically knows what will turn his partner on. His partner has to teach him. Also, not having learned about themselves fosters passivity in women. And passivity breeds anxiety. If you're passive in sex, you're being "done to," not in control and possibly tense because you don't really know what's going to happen next. On the other hand, assertiveness competes with and inhibits anxiety. So, to be active in sex helps make you comfortable, relaxed and involved.

A lack of sex (not masturbating when other outlets are not possible or wanted) can cause pelvic congestion. It's ironic, considering the appalling things that masturbation has been accused of causing, to note that its lack can cause backache, tension, edginess, irritability, insomnia and headaches.

Well, enough of the origins and history of masturbation's unfortunate reputation. I simply wanted to air the myths and lower anxiety and apprehension about self-exploration. After all, most people do it, and it's normal and enjoyable. And, to return to the main point of this chapter, masturbation is therapeutic in orgasmic reconditioning. Orgasmic reconditioning won't work unless you are aroused. Anxiety and guilt inhibit arousal, so it is important that you are relaxed to diminish any guilt or anxiety you might feel about masturbation after all I have said. Usually words, however rational, logical, sensible and authoritative, are not enough to overcome early conditioning. If you still feel uneasy about masturbation, there's an activity in the exercise section of this chapter that you should find useful.

The next question to be answered, then, is do you need to learn orgasmic reconditioning and if so, how is it done?

If you still feel physically attracted to your former partner, if you would feel more than a little anxious or guilty about relating physically to someone new, then you could find orgasmic reconditioning helpful. It's an easy technique to explain for males and a little more complicated for females.

If you're male, masturbate to a fantasy of your former lover. (You might use her picture. Or imagine making love to her on the beach. Or recall one of the first times you made love together, or one of the best.) At the next to the last possible moment, just before orgasm, switch to visualizing the new person and continue picturing the new person on through orgasm. The "last possible moment before orgasm" needs a word of explanation.

Just before a male has an orgasm, he reaches a level of excitement called the point of inevitability. Once he reaches that point, he will go on to orgasm no matter what happens. The mounted police could break down the door and ride into the room on horseback and the man would still go on to orgasm. Generally this point of inevitability occurs one to five seconds before orgasm. There is no equivalent phenomenon in females. A slight sound such as a baby's cough from another room or a stray thought can at any time interrupt a woman's sexual excitement and prevent orgasm. This physiological difference makes orgasmic reconditioning simpler for a man than for a woman.

So the first time you masturbate to an image or fantasy of your former lover, switch to imagining your new partner at the last possible moment before orgasm. The next time you masturbate, switch your fantasy three to four seconds earlier, and each successive time, keep switching earlier and 107 earlier. Keep backing up in time until you can start from the beginning with a fantasy of the new person. If your arousal should diminish, you have gone back too quickly. Orgasmic reconditioning takes from one week to three months depending on your own masturbatory patterns, the levels of guilt and/or anxiety that have to be overcome, and your state of mind and how attracted you are to the new person in the first place. It is important to take all the time you need.

Here is one example of a man who successfully went through orgasmic reconditioning:

•

Andrew, thirty-nine-year-old grocery store owner. Andrew's wife died. He had been very fond of her and went through a period of grief and depression. For a little over three months he felt no sexual desire, which is quite normal in periods of grief and depression. About a year later, Andrew began seeing another woman. She was his age and had been divorced. They often went bowling together and went out to dinner and the movies together every weekend. They had many things to share, but Andrew felt no physical desire for her. She was a warm, affectionate person, but he felt guilty about kissing her. "It was almost like being unfaithful," he said. They went to bed together three times, but Andrew could not get an erection. She was understanding, he said, but he felt humiliated. When he asked for my help, he said he was seriously considering breaking off the relationship although it meant a great deal to him, and he felt he was in love with her. In doing orgasmic reconditioning, Andrew would masturbate picturing himself making love to his former wife while they were on a camping trip together, and then, at the point of inevitability, he would switch to imagining himself making love to his new partner as he had an orgasm. Over a period of three weeks, he would switch to a fantasy of his new partner a few seconds earlier each time until he was able to imagine making love to her from the beginning of his masturbation all the way through orgasm. Andrew was then able to make love with his new partner.

•

Some neurological researchers believe that orgasm stimulates the septal region of the brain, causing feelings of warmth and affection (and reduction of anger) for your real or imagined partner.

In switching to a new partner, in your mind, while masturbating, and then experiencing orgasm with that new partner in your imagination, you tend to increase your feelings of affection and desire for the new partner and to decrease your guilt and anxiety about having a sexual relationship with a new person. Orgasm also has a powerful conditioning effect here, because you associate the new person with a peak of intense pleasure.

Women usually find orgasmic reconditioning more difficult for three reasons. Fewer women masturbate, and fewer women are orgasmic than men. And women, as I mentioned, do not have that point of inevitability, that "Aha, no matter what happens, I am going to have an orgasm." So a woman has to wait until she is into an orgasm before she can switch images of her partner. This is far from easy. The sudden intrusion of a new partner, even in fantasy, may be disrupting. So it takes more practice for women than for men. But the technique itself is very similar. You begin to masturbate with the fantasy of your old lover (or to another fantasy if that is easier), and you switch to your new partner as you first begin to have an orgasm. Then, each successive time you masturbate, you back up the "switch" a little bit to just before orgasm, until you can begin masturbating on through to orgasm with an image of your new partner. If you find that touching yourself is not very stimulating, you may find that reading a book that turns you on will be helpful in arousing your excitement. Many women find that books like *The Pearl* (an anonymous Victorian journal), 109

The Betsy (Harold Robbins), *My Secret Garden* (Nancy Friday), and *Delta of Venus* (Anaïs Nin) make arousing, erotic reading.

You may prefer something else, such as a warm bath or soft music or even all three. Here's one woman who had a very good experience with orgasmic reconditioning:

•

Linda, twenty-six-year-old mother, married to a policeman. Her husband was a solid, serious man, devoted to his daughter and to Linda. But in contrast to the man she was having an affair with, Linda's husband seemed dull. Her lover was a part-time mechanic and sometime racing car driver, a wonderful storyteller and a strong, demanding lover. However, Linda felt it was a dead-end affair and wanted to stay in her marriage. We did thought-stopping to get her mind off her lover, and we did orgasmic reconditioning to regain her sexual attraction to her husband. Linda was strongly orgasmic and had practiced masturbation since she was thirteen, so orgasmic reconditioning was relatively easy for her. In doing the technique she recalled her first lovemaking experience with her husband before they were married. And she also fantasized about new ways and new places that she and her husband might make love. She and her husband had fallen into a set pattern in their lovemaking. Like so many people, they had the habit of waiting until the very end of the evening when they were both tired and sleepy to engage in the intensely emotional, creative and physical act of making love. So I suggested that they vary the pattern to make love at noon on the weekends, before dinner when possible. And I urged them to take a sensual holiday. They found that outside their apartment, away from the child and the ordinary pressures of bills to pay and the neighbor's too-loud television, they could rediscover the passion, inventiveness, spontaneity, and relaxed, warm lovemaking that they had once enjoyed.

Exercises

For Men

1. Masturbate to a fantasy of your former lover.
2. Just before orgasm, at the point of inevitability, switch to a fantasy of your new lover, and continue on to orgasm.
3. Next time you masturbate, switch your fantasy three to four seconds earlier.
4. Each successive time you masturbate, switch your fantasy earlier and earlier until you can masturbate from start to finish picturing the new person.

For Women

1. Masturbate to a fantasy of your former lover.
2. At the first second of orgasm, switch to imagining making love with the new person.
3. Next time you masturbate, switch your fantasy three to four seconds earlier.
4. Each successive time you masturbate, switch your fantasy earlier and earlier until you can masturbate from start to finish, picturing the new person.

If You Feel Mildly Anxious about Masturbation

1. Find a quiet comfortable place where you know you won't be disturbed.
2. Read a book or a magazine article or look at some pictures that you find sensual and arousing.
3. When you are in the midst of feeling sensual, touch yourself for a few seconds or until you feel very slightly uncomfortable.

111

4. Then go back to the book or article or pictures until you are relaxed, feeling sensual again without feeling any anxiety.

Note: Erotic feelings are not as strong an inhibitor of anxiety as is deep relaxation. Anxiety can easily interfere with arousal. Therefore you need to move into self-stimulation cautiously and gradually, always making sure that the erotic feelings are stronger than your anxiety. That way you can learn, emotionally, to feel relaxed and erotic instead of anxious.

5. Repeat steps three and four several times, each time touching yourself for a few seconds longer, or until you just feel very slightly anxious.

6. Repeat steps one through four as many or as few times a week as you wish until you can touch yourself, and feel aroused, without feeling anxious.

Note: If you feel strongly anxious about masturbation, and you wish to overcome this feeling, you may need the help of a behavior therapist. You might also want to read Lonnie Barbach's excellent book, *For Yourself.*

9

Sexuality—A New Beginning

We are sexual creatures. The intricate interplay between two people is full of sexual themes, overtones and undertones. You know more about sex than you did at the beginning of your old relationship. And now you have a chance to be brand-new again without stumbling over your old mistakes or falling into old selfish patterns. And because of the wonderful possibilities of a fresh start, it is important to give the sexual part of your new relationship every possible advantage. There's no shortage of sexual advice. Bookstores have whole departments devoted to the subject. But much of it is centered on performance. If you are at all worried about that, a book emphasizing performance will increase your anxiety rather than help it. Oddly enough, the less you are concerned about performance (erection, lubrication, excitement, orgasm), the less likely it is that it's going to be a problem. Of course, once you are concerned about performance, it is very difficult not to worry about it. What you need to do is learn anew to focus on other areas, on pleasure, on giving and receiving pleasure. And that is what I am going to teach you to do. Making love is indeed the creation of love. It is a creative act. The love you feel for one another is infinitely more important and satisfying than any combination of techniques. And yet, because making love is an expression of love, a   113 mutual creative act as well as a learned one, there is every reason to want to make that expression as loving, caring and eloquent as possible. So now I'd like to make some specific constructive suggestions about how you can increase your own and your partner's self-assurance, pleasure and communication.

Several of the techniques outlined in the sensual holiday section will give you and your partner more pleasure; bans, asking for sensual things, focusing on sensation instead of performance, bathing together, teasing, teaching, setting the mood, and seduction are all helpful. In addition, I have other suggestions to make. But first, I'd like you to take a slow, relaxed look at sexual response, how and why it happens. It's more than an interesting subject. Intensifying your sensual pleasure is a way to feel better about yourself and to improve your capacity for loving. The more pleasure you feel, the more pleasure you can give. Only recently have we been able to learn what really happens during sex and why. There's still a great deal of mystery, but knowing some of the whys, what causes what and the nature of the link between this and that can make you a more caring, considerate and complete lover. Back in the fifties, Masters and Johnson observed thousands of people making love. They took movies of lovemaking, they interviewed the lovers and they recorded their findings with precision and care. Add to that all the observations, surveys and discoveries of all the other sex researchers over the past twenty years and what emerges is a fairly clear picture of what happens, physically, during sex.

Arousal

You begin to feel attracted and excited and being touched and touching turns you on. You feel desire, a compelling need to be close and physically involved. You begin to breathe faster. Your pulse rate rises. Blood rushes into your genitals faster than it goes out, so the penis becomes erect and the clitoris enlarges. (Clitoral enlargement varies. It may be hardly noticeable.) You may perspire and become flushed, and your muscles may tense as you feel increasingly excited. The sexual organs become unusually sensitive to touch. Testicles rise toward the body as the scrotal skin becomes tense and thick. The interior of the vagina begins to turn a darker pink and lubricate with a pearly fluid as the uterus begins to lift off the floor of the vaginal barrel. As excitement increases, the interior two thirds of the vagina go through waves of expansion and relaxation, becoming larger as if to make room for the penis. The penis becomes more sensitive, with the tip becoming extremely sensitive. The inner lips of the vagina swell and deepen in color to a rich, rosy plum. The female breasts enlarge as much as 25 percent, nipples become erect and sensitive. The penis may emit a clear liquid as a lubricant. (This liquid usually contains a small amount of sperm, which means that withdrawal before orgasm is no guarantee of contraception.)

Breathing and pulse rates continue to increase. Blood pressure rises. Muscle tension becomes stronger and stronger. Women may show a blotchy measleslike (maculopapular) flush over the legs, thighs and pelvic area. Lying on your back, you may experience carpopedal spasms (both men and women), which means your toes curl up. The inner two thirds of the vagina continue to enlarge and become smoother, but the outer one third becomes smaller and tighter, increasing the sensation between a thrusting penis and the outer vagina. The clitoris retracts under a clitoral hood. In intercourse, the thrusting of the penis pulls the inner lips of the vagina, which in turn pulls the clitoral hood over the clitoris. It's this back and forth movement of the clitoral hood over the clitoris that produces a great part of the female stimulation during intercourse. (Contrary to 115 popular belief, there are not two kinds of female orgasm. Female orgasm is almost always the result of direct and/or indirect clitoral stimulation.) Lubrication from the vaginal walls and from the penis continues and even increases. Just before orgasm the smaller lips of the vagina turn bright pink or a deeper rosy red. Muscle tension builds and builds.

Orgasm

Some 75 percent of men reach orgasm within two minutes of direct genital stimulation. Some 75 percent of women take longer. It is not at all uncommon for a woman to need at least fourteen minutes to reach orgasm. A man and woman rarely reach a simultaneous orgasm. That is why trying to achieve it can be frustrating, make you both anxious, and is beside the point.

In orgasm a great many things happen in such quick succession that it seems as if it's all happening at once. Blood pressure, pulse rate and breathing rate all reach a peak. The reddish sex flush on the skin (25 percent of men and most women have it) is at its highest point. Your hands may clench and grasp. The muscles in your arms, legs, feet and neck contract in a spasm. In a man's body, liquid from several different glands begins to flow into and collect in a bulb in the prostate gland. The fluid, collectively, is called semen. And it is at this point, as the semen builds up pressure, that a man knows he is going to ejaculate. Within one to five seconds after the seminal fluids gather in the prostatic bulb, muscles at the base of the penis contract, in three to four successive waves occurring every four fifths of a second, and propel the seminal fluid through the penis and out in a rush accompanied by an intense, sometimes almost unbearable excitement, pleasure and release. In a woman the outer third of the vagina contracts in a suc-

116

cession of rhythmic waves at intervals of four fifths of a second, faster than she could contract those muscles voluntarily. The uterus also contracts rhythmically. She has three to twelve contractions accompanied by many different feelings of intensity, pleasure and euphoria originating in the clitoral and vaginal area and often flowing through the whole body. Both men and women may experience muscular jerking, arching, groaning, grasping, shouting, grimacing and writhing.

Afterglow

In men orgasm is followed by an almost immediate release of muscular tension and an abrupt draining of blood out of the penis and pelvic region. The penis returns to its usual size and a man is, usually, relaxed and even sleepy. In contrast, a woman comes down very gradually. Some women, with varying kinds of stimulation, can go on from orgasm to orgasm, feeling more or feeling less pleasure with each successive orgasm. In any case, biologically, a woman usually experiences a much longer afterglow, a lingering feeling of warmth and pleasure. Men, on the other hand, enter another phase called the refractory, in which another orgasm cannot happen. An erection may or may not appear during this phase (which lasts anywhere from a few minutes to hours or days) but an orgasm is simply not physically possible.

I am very much aware that the foregoing is no more than a rough blueprint of what happens during lovemaking. Like a blueprint of, say, a grand cathedral organ, the broad outlines are there, and there are indications of the functions of the stops and pipes, but the music is missing. Missing too are the infinite variations of texture, shape, smell, taste and emotion and the whole substance of love, what we feel for one another. Certainly it's helpful to know the organic   117 functions of the human organism. But I want to be extremely careful not to mislead you as do so many of the current crop of sex manuals. Of course, there are an extraordinary variety of positions and techniques. But there is no right way or wrong way. Far more important than any technique or exercise or position is knowing both your own needs and desires and being able to recognize and respond to the needs and desires of the person you are with. Here, then, are several ideas to help you know your own needs, to help you communicate with your partner, and to help you understand, appreciate and respond to your partner with love.

1. *Caring.* Show your love with touches and caresses. Be considerate. Make love *with* someone, not *to* someone.

2. *Getting Started* (for women). Some women find it helpful to relax before making love because relaxation reduces anxiety. A warm bath, soft music, touching yourself, fantasizing or reading an arousing book can all help reduce anxiety and increase the pleasure and intensity of your lovemaking. Fantasy can be a great pleasure. You might like to think of lovers you'd like to have, erotic situations, places you'd like to be while making love, and dreams from childhood. Fantasizing is certainly not a necessary thing to do, but if you'd like an idea of other women's fantasies, *My Secret Garden* by Nancy Friday is a good collection. The point is that for some reason — and I don't know precisely why — for a good many women, the hardest thing is getting started. Reading erotic books is arousing for many women. Setting the mood, relaxing a little, can also help a woman to arrive at the lovemaking experience already aroused. For some women, it is well worth the extra time it takes to be aroused before lovemaking begins.

3. *Masturbating* (for women). In my experience, there is no such thing as a "frigid" woman. Orgasm is learned, not

automatic. And some women have not yet learned. These women are not "frigid," they are simply preorgasmic. It's beyond the scope of this book to teach you how to have an orgasm; however, everything mentioned here is helpful. What I would like to do is to raise the level of your enjoyment. As with men, the best advice I can give you to learn about your own senses, desires and pleasures is to touch yourself. Masturbate. Begin with clitoral stimulation at the top of the inner vaginal lips. See how you like to be touched, directly or indirectly, softly or with a firm touch. Touch other parts of your body, your stomach, thighs and/or vaginal area. If you find yourself getting bored or beginning to focus on your performance as opposed to what you feel, stop and relax. Do something else for a while and come back to touching yourself later.

One way to lose anxiety about performance is to make a contract with yourself not to have an orgasm. Focus instead on a specific sensation in your shoulder, thigh or, say, hands. Applying a lubricant to the clitoral or vaginal area may also be helpful in increasing your pleasure. Many women report that Koromex II jelly (a spermicidal jelly usually used with a diaphragm) or even hand lotion not only feels good, it relieves their anxiety about whether or not they have enough lubrication.

4. *Slowing Down* (mainly for men). Perhaps the single most important thing men can do to increase the pleasure of their lovemaking is to learn to slow down. Slow down at the beginning of lovemaking. And slow down during intercourse. Teasing and delaying produces a much greater build-up and a stronger release. It's much more loving and pleasurable to take your time and enjoy all the sensations along the way.

If you frequently have a premature ejaculation, Dr. James Semans has developed a technique that can help 119 you delay ejaculation. You'll find the Semans technique, which he developed in 1955 at Duke University, in the exercise section at the end of this chapter.

5. *No Goal.* I think "foreplay" is a misleading term. It implies that something better is going to happen later. But intercourse isn't better so much as it is different. A great part of the pleasure of lovemaking is in the hugging and kissing and fondling. That's when you get to share sensations and build up a feeling of intimacy and sexual excitement between the two of you. Let go of thinking of orgasm or intercourse as the goal you are striving for and simply enjoy the infinite variety of pleasure you can give each other right now. A ban on intercourse for an afternoon or evening helps develop a no goal attitude and it can heighten your excitement and expectation as well as help break the pattern of "quick entry."

6. *Separate Focus* (for men). Focus on a specific sensation outside your genital area while you are caressing each other, a tingling in the toes, for example, or a warmth in your thighs. The idea of being alert to all of your sensations is partly to increase your own pleasure, and partly to become less concerned with your performance. So much of our culture seems to suggest that the most important part of a man's lovemaking is the duration and frequency of his erection. This, of course, is nonsense. As Dr. William Kirby has pointed out, even if you don't have an erection, you have ten erect fingers. In other words, you will be a more loving, caring partner if you relax about your performance. Dr. Kirby adds, "Be a lover, not a scorekeeper."

7. *Assertiveness.* Being assertive (asking for what you'd like, showing, teaching) reduces anxiety. Anxiety blocks pleasure. So being assertive not only gets you what you want, it increases the pleasure you feel. And

it helps your partner to know what you want and do not want.

8. *The Clitoris.* Clitoral stimulation is usually essential for female arousal. As you no doubt know, there is no preferred or magic technique for clitoral stimulation. The best technique for each woman is the one she prefers for herself. A man has to learn how a woman wants to be touched. A woman has to teach her partner how she wants to be touched. It can be delicious for both of you.

9. *Lotions and Oils.* Lotions and oils can help you spend more time touching, massaging and loving each other. They are particularly nice in genital stimulation. And they can remove a woman's anxiety about lubrication. Stay away from perfumed lotions. Koromex II jelly, Keri Lotion, baby oil and baby lotion are all fine.

10. *Almosting.* Going right up to and then backing away from orgasm can increase its intensity. Stop short of orgasm several times during lovemaking. You'll need to talk about this with your partner if you'd like to try it.

11. *Vaginal Exercise* (for women). Another excellent exercise to intensify your pleasure and to increase the quality of your orgasm is vaginal muscle contraction as suggested by Dr. Arnold Kegel, an obstetrician in California. The muscle that stops and starts the flow of urine is also the muscle that contracts during orgasm. If you can make that muscle stronger, you may have the pleasure of more intense feelings during orgasm. You can begin practicing contracting that muscle during urination with your knees about one foot apart. Simply become aware of the muscle and notice that you can contract and relax it at will. You can begin contracting the muscle ten times a day. You may find it difficult to do at first, but if you work up to a hundred contractions a day you may find that you can have deeper, more powerful orgasms. 121

Next contract and relax the muscle as you masturbate during clitoral and vaginal stimulation. As the contraction becomes easier to do, you might try contracting it around your finger until you can do it rapidly, almost fluttering, or slowly. You might then try doing these muscle contractions around your partner's penis when the penis is either holding still or moving very slowly. This can feel wonderful for both of you.

12. *Movement* (for women). Pelvic movement contributes to the intensity of your orgasm. Some women do not experience an orgasm if they don't move their pelvis. And some women prefer to "be on top" so that they can better control their pelvic movement and stimulation.

13. *Noise.* Making noise releases tension and lets you let yourself go. Shout, yowl, moan and sigh if you feel like doing so. It is a great way to increase your pleasure. Be a sonic boom even.

14. *Clitoral Stimulation during Intercourse* (for women). To repeat, every woman is different. There is no right or wrong way. A woman can intensify her pleasure by showing her partner how she prefers being touched. Clitoral stimulation during intercourse often adds to a woman's pleasure. Either her own or her partner's hand, whichever she prefers.

15. *Muscle Tension.* Muscle tension is a part of orgasm, as you have seen. Tensing your thigh muscles just before orgasm can produce a small increase in the strength of your orgasm. A little bondage — playfully holding your partner's hands down while you tease and stimulate your partner — if you both agree to it and feel comfortable with it, can enhance muscle tension.

16. *Variety.* Make love in a different way, in a different place, at a different time. It's absurd to always save the intensely creative, energetic, emotional experience for

the last thing of the day before you go to sleep. There's a great deal to be said for "matinees."

Sex is such an overheated subject that I feel I should add another point. The techniques I have discussed for improving your enjoyment should be just that, enjoyable. You certainly should not do any of them that make you feel guilty or anxious. After all, for all its taboos, intricacies, mysteries and pleasures, sex is only part of your life. And it is only part of relating to yourself and to someone you love.

Exercises (for Men)

The Semans Technique for Delaying Ejaculation

1. Masturbate until *just before* you reach the point of inevitability, where you go to ejaculation within one to five seconds.
2. Stop and rest until you can take more stimulation without ejaculating.
3. Masturbate again until, once again, you reach a point just before the point of inevitability.
4. Stop and rest again until you can take more stimulation without ejaculating.
5. Masturbate, and stop and rest again. Then masturbate on through to ejaculation.
6. Repeat steps one through five, four to six times a week for two weeks.
7. After two weeks repeat the process using K-Y jelly or Koromex II jelly or a body lotion so that masturbation feels more like the inside of a vagina . . . stopping and resting, masturbating just up to the point before inevitability, and resting again.

In two more weeks you will find that it is beginning to take longer to reach the point of inevitability. And you'll find that you will be able to identify that point with certainty. Not only will you find that it's taking you longer to reach orgasm, you'll also learn how to pace yourself.

When you make love with a partner, practice moving slowly and with partial penetration. You might ask your partner to hold still for a while or slow down. You might also withdraw before point of inevitability and rest before resuming again. (It's important to point out that you need to maintain a high frequency of sex, supplementing intercourse with masturbation if necessary, so you ejaculate several times a week.)

124

10

In Love

An endnote.

Remember when you were a child, getting out of school for summer vacation? The summer seemed so long you couldn't see to the end of it. And remember being back in school in the autumn when there was an eternity to endure before spring? From your viewpoint it may seem that there will never be another love in your life. Time holds us captive at any given moment. But seasons come and go. And summers and loves grow smaller in the distance of time passed. Your old love is past now. The future is full of change.

You may well feel you will never fall in love again. And who knows, you may be right. But the odds are against your staying out of love. For one thing, you're wiser now. Now that you are less dominated by thoughts of another person you are a larger personality in the best sense. And now that you have the techniques of positive image building you can see and appreciate yourself in the best sense. As you are more positive about yourself, other people will also see you in a better light and appreciate you more. Sexuality and sensuality are important, but they are only part of loving. Given the techniques and attitudes discussed in the previous chapters, you can now give your love more range and expression. Just as the techniques of falling out of love are learned, so too is falling in love. You learn to be in love with someone. And you learn through being accepted and affirmed by someone. It's emotional learning. You can't decide to be in love with someone, work at it and then find yourself in love. "He's good-looking and successful, I'll fall in love with him." Love is simply too emotional to be preplanned.

When you do fall in love again, often it is better the second time. Because it is a new chance to begin again on a new base of a greater wisdom and experience. For each of us love is different each time. There's a magical interplay of hormones, senses and emotions that gives you a high, an intensity, an elation, a sense of well-being and just feeling good. Always it is a different high, a different feel-good feeling. But however magical the feelings, there is also a hard reality. Sooner or later the electric excitement of a new love's newness wears off. Sooner or later there will be problems. The most common problems stem from believing the childish fairy tale that one day you will find your perfect, perfect person, the one who will be right for you in every way. It's an impossibly high hope that always leads to disappointment and broken relationships. There is no perfect person for you. One person cannot fulfill all your needs and expectations. And it is an unfair burden to expect them to carry. However, as you become more assertive, you also become more self-sufficient and less dependent. One person doesn't have to fulfill all your needs because you can fulfill some of them yourself. Ah, but being in love does fulfill fantasies. Whether it's moonlight walks and talks or simply feeling safe at home in bed with a warm, loving person kissing you good night, love is the time and the place where you get to do lots of those playful, romantic, sexy things you wanted to.

A definition of love as giving and sharing means that you do not exploit the other person. It's so easy to make demands or be critical, but less easy when another person's needs are as important to you as your own. To be sure, there are plenty of people in love who play destructive or manipulative roles. But that's not helpful to either partner. And usually we see one person being exploited, diminished and even damaged.

The best of love is a total acceptance of another person; an acceptance of weaknesses, mistakes and vulnerabilities along with the goodnesses and strengths. Accepting and being accepted means that you are free to be yourself in a relationship. You don't have to play a role or feel you have to change yourself or your partner into someone slightly different. In love you get to be your best in a very broad sense, emotionally, physically, mentally, in every way.

When you are in love, you save your best for that relationship. You can realize your potential in areas that you just can't realize anywhere else in life. You can realize your potential for giving, loving, caring, being beautiful, sexual, tender, helpful and on and on.

In love you can give without asking for anything in return.

Index

Index

131